THE UK

NO FLY
Cruising

An independent expert guide to the UK 'no fly' Cruise market

by

Marc Jones & Ernie Skalsky

NO FLY CRUISING.com

Published in Great Britain in 2011 by
Cruise Experts Limited, Coast Road, Hopton-on-Sea, Norfolk NR31 9BX
Tel: 0844 856 9471
info@noflycruising.com
www.noflycruising.com

Cover photography kindly supplied by MSC Cruises ⚙ **MSC** _{CRUISES}
© 2011 MSC Crociere S.A. All rights reserved.

Cover design and typeset by Stuart Hawes

Printed and bound in Great Britain by:
Micropress
Tel: 01986 834200
www.micropress.co.uk

British Library Cataloguing in Publications Data.
ISBN: 978-0-9568541-0-0

The UK Guide to No Fly Cruising

Content

Foreword 4

Introduction 5

The benefits of 'no fly' cruising 7

Which 'no fly' cruise is right for you? 10
When are you planning to travel?
Where do you want to go?
How long do you want your 'no fly' cruise to be?
What style of 'no fly' cruise would best suit you?
What's your budget?

The main 'no-fly' Cruise Lines & ships 24

UK 'no fly' cruising departure ports 56

How to get the best deal on your 'no fly' cruise holiday 64
How to read the Cruise Lines' brochures
Who's who in the selling game
The discount maze
5 Handy Hints to follow when booking your 'no fly' cruise

Life on board 73

16 things that the glossy brochures won't tell you 84

The 10 classic objections to cruising 87

Frequently asked questions 89

Where to go for further information 94

Foreword

If you are anything like us, you will have heard an increasing number of friends, relatives and colleagues discussing cruising as an exciting holiday alternative. In the past cruising as a holiday appeared to only be the choice of the fairly mature who were more than fairly well off. Now, there is a cruise for everyone and almost every taste; families, couples, singles, bridge players, dancers, music or sports lovers, history & world affairs, wellness, political, nature, cultural, lifestyle, food and wine through to those seeking nothing but pure relaxation or for others fun and entertainment including star studded stage shows afloat.

The ships are also more spacious, even more luxurious and ever more interesting places to be as the industry invests literally billions in creating these impressive floating resorts. They aim to provide everything that a land based resort has to offer, turning the journey into as much part of the holiday as the destinations themselves. In addition, whereas the land based resort holiday is traditionally centred on one location, a cruise holiday has an almost limitless choice of destinations and itineraries.

More often than not however, potential cruisers are confused by the choice on offer and are turned off by the competing advertising claims in the press and online. Reading the pages upon pages of cruise adverts in the Sunday papers can be a bewildering experience that confuses rather than clarifies.

And with so many cruise options available it is no surprise that the market is so confusing. Approximately 40% of all UK cruisers choose to cruise from a UK port on a 'no fly' cruise holiday. It is the most popular cruise option for new cruisers, as well as more mature cruisers and this is why No Fly Cruising.com (www.noflycruising.com) was launched.

No Fly Cruising.com offers expert guidance solely on the UK 'no fly' cruise market. We deliberately do not sell any cruise that does not depart from and return to a UK port and this ensures that we know the 'no fly' cruise market inside out. And because we are independent from any Cruise Line we can offer unbiased advice that puts you, the holidaymaker, first.

The UK Guide to No Fly Cruising is not intended to be an exhaustive analysis of the market, more a steer in the right direction. So, if after reading you feel that 'no fly' cruising is the perfect solution for you then please feel free to give us a call to discuss your individual requirements in more detail.

Marc Jones & Ernie Skalsky
No Fly Cruising.com

Introduction

In the last ten years the number of people choosing a cruise for their main holiday has increased dramatically to the point where now, in 2010, one in every ten package holidays booked is a cruise.

Cruising has continued to increase despite the political upheaval following 9/11 and the worldwide recession after the banking crisis.

Yet with more and more people looking at cruising for their next holiday it is clear that the industry is in danger of shooting itself in the foot when it comes to presenting to new cruisers clear, concise and relevant information.

Open any Sunday newspaper and there are hundreds of cruise companies, travel agents and tour operators claiming that their cruise has the best itinerary, is on the best ship, operated by the best Cruise Line and offered to you at the best price. But how do you really make sense of all these competing claims? After all, they can't all be the best, can they?

If you go on the web and type in cruise(s) and cruising, Google will throw up some 102,000,000 total results making it practically impossible for anyone who does not work in the industry to make sense of all that.

In addition, pretty much all of the official and unofficial independent guides available to buy, are written by Americans for the American market, with web-based information for the UK market only offered by individual Cruise Lines which can hardly claim to be 'independent'.

This is why this guide has been written, because we believe that those interested in cruise holidays need better information, not just better offers. No matter how many extras you get and how big a discount you are offered, it won't be a good deal if the cruise you select is not right for you.

This is also the reason why this guide is exclusively about 'no fly' cruising from UK ports. It deals with the cruises that research suggests are the most popular and fastest growing choice amongst UK residents. This is therefore written exclusively for the UK market which will save you having to plough through the majority of information out there that really is irrelevant to everyone living outside of the USA.

So, what is 'no fly' cruising?

Well, 'no fly' cruising is the industry definition for cruises that depart from and return to a UK port. And currently about 40% of UK cruise passengers choose a 'no fly' cruise. They are particularly popular with first time cruisers, but are also becoming increasingly popular with regular cruisers who find the convenience, flexibility, variety and value attractive.

In 2011 alone twenty-one Cruise Lines, operating 40 ships depart from and return to UK ports on a total of 506 cruises. So which one will be perfect for you?

The UK guide to 'no fly' cruising is designed to provide you with the right information with which to make an informed choice as to which cruise is right for you depending upon your key individual requirements:

O *When are you planning to travel?*
O *Where do you want to go?*
O *How long do you want your 'no fly' cruise to be?*
O *What style of 'no fly' cruise would best suit you and your party?*
O *What's your budget?*

There are sections on the *main 'no fly' Cruise Lines and ships*, the *main destinations* served by the UK 'no fly' cruise ships dependent on duration, information on the *main UK 'no fly' cruise ports*, what to expect when you're *on-board*, how to get *the best deal for your cruise*, plus a handy *frequently asked questions* chapter.

By the end of this guide we hope that you will be better informed and more confident in determining which 'no fly' cruise will be right for you, but if you do need to explore further then our *where to go for further information* section will point you in the right direction.

Happy 'no fly' cruising!

The benefits of 'no fly' cruising

Of course there are many reasons why people choose to cruise rather than go on alternative land based resort holidays:

O *It's a hassle-free holiday*
O *It takes you away from it all*
O *You'll never have the opportunity to be more pampered*
O *You can visit a broad geographical area in one trip*
O *A cruise offers huge variety in activities, dining and entertainment*
O *It's an ideal place to make new friends*
O *It's the perfect romantic holiday*
O *There's a cruise to appeal to every taste*
O *A cruise is one of the safest ways to travel*
O *It represents fabulous value for money*

However, it is no surprise that the popularity of 'no fly' cruising continues to grow as there are a number of factors in its favour that are particularly attractive to cruise virgins and experienced cruisers alike.

'No fly' cruising is convenient

We live on an island and with no town more than 70 miles from the sea it is easy to get to one of the major ports. Even with the major sailings from the south coast the UK rail and road infrastructure makes getting to ports relatively easy and certainly considerably easier than flying abroad!

All of the major ports have invested in secure car parking facilities and all the major Cruise Lines make the transfer from car to ship as painless as possible.

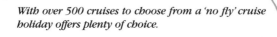

With over 500 cruises to choose from a 'no fly' cruise holiday offers plenty of choice.

It's safe

The Cruise Lines have invested heavily in security to ensure the safety and comfort of their passengers and this has certainly been shown in recent surveys that compare cruises favourably against other forms of travel. But above all else Cruise Lines have an enviable safety record when compared to all other forms of transportation.

You don't have to fly

Not unsurprisingly this is the most important reason as to why 'no fly' cruising is becoming increasingly popular. Airport delays, cost (including the increasing level and variety of departure and so called 'green' taxes), concerns over safety and worries over luggage all work in favour of 'no fly' cruising.

You don't have to suffer airports.

Of course less time queuing and dealing with noisy departure lounges make cruises from the UK a perfect option for families where there are young children. The hassle free process of arriving at the departure port and boarding your ship are bound to keep you, but more importantly, the little ones happy; the perfect start for family cruises.

You don't have to put up with 'low cost' service

With low cost airlines grabbing such a large slice of the market, most of us have experienced the misery of cramped seating, lack of customer service and 'extra' charges for everything from luggage to refreshments. A 'no fly' cruise avoids all of this ensuring that your holiday commences as soon as you reach your UK departure port.

There are no luggage limitations

Another reason why regular cruisers prefer to 'no fly' is that they are able to take as much luggage as they wish on board. After all, it's pretty difficult to get all your packing into one bag of less than 20kg at the best of times. If you are embarking on a longer cruise the restriction on weight becomes a pressing (and potentially expensive) issue if you have to pass through airport check-ins. Each Cruise Line has a slightly different policy, but as a guide up to 90kg is generally perfectly acceptable!

You only go through security once

On all foreign holiday and fly cruises you are obliged to go through airport security up to four times (twice on the way out and twice on the way back). On a cruise this only happens once, at your departure port in the UK, cutting down on aggravation, stress and queuing!

Your holiday starts immediately

At your UK departure port your luggage is generally taken from you where you park or as you enter the departure hall – you then go through security and passport control and only see your luggage again in your cabin. And once onboard ship your holiday begins immediately because on a cruise your destination is just another stage in your itinerary, your journey is all part of the holiday by design.

Your holiday is the same length as the cruise duration

If you book a 7 day 'no fly' cruise you arrive at the UK port on your first day and you arrive back to the UK on your last day, maximising your holiday time.

Unlike 'fly' cruises, you do not have to factor in travel time to an airport, check-in times, flight time, time-zone changes and extra time for potential delays that, without taking into consideration, could see you arrive at your port of departure to see your ship sailing off into the horizon. And in such a circumstance be under no illusions, it is you who is responsible for the costs of getting to the next port of call in order to join your cruise. So to ensure that this eventuality does not happen many fly cruises recommend that you arrive in your city of departure the day before your cruise departs, adding further hotel costs to your holiday expenditure.

You sail with like minded passengers

On a 'no fly' cruise the vast majority of your fellow cruisers will be British. The cruises are designed to appeal to the culinary and cultural tastes of British citizens, so you will be sailing with fellow travellers who are likely to have shared values and interests to those of your own.

It's great value for money

With cruises from the UK you start your holiday the moment you board the ship, giving you even more time to enjoy your holiday. And without the cost of flights to take into consideration the value for money of a 'no fly' cruise stands out.

When you are looking at a 'no fly' cruise for the first time you need to take into consideration all of the costs of an alternative holiday option when making a value comparison. Then, when comparing, you will see that a 'no fly' cruising holiday represents a superb value for money option.

> *Starting and finishing your cruise in the UK provides you with a far more relaxed holiday*

Which 'no fly' cruise is right for you?

This section asks five key questions that you need to have in mind to ensure that the cruise you eventually choose is the right one for you. After all, no matter how budget minded you are, a cruise is not a cheap holiday and although it can offer tremendous value for money, it can only be considered 'cheap' if it is compared to a land based holiday option of equal inclusiveness and quality.

> *When comparing to a land based holiday always take into consideration that all your meals, entertainment and most activities and facilities are included in your cruise price*

The huge increase in cruising and the introduction of more and more ships into the market has now opened this great experience up to everyone. The days of cruising being the preserve of the privileged few is long gone and no matter who you are *(a family, romantic couple, party animal, culture vulture, sophisticated senior, adventurous single or fanatical bridge player)* there is a perfect cruise waiting for you.

Five key questions that 'no fly' cruising virgins need to consider

The five questions that follow are inter-related and so it would be useful to consider the questions as a whole rather than individually.

Question 1: When are you planning to travel?

If you are planning to cruise during the winter months then you are looking at longer cruise durations as the ships tend to travel to more temperate climates. Your choice is also going to be restricted as fewer ships sail in northern Europe at this time of year, preferring to operate on the other side of the world until the European spring comes. But there are cruises departing from the UK every month of the year so ask your 'no fly' cruise specialist for information on specific dates if your decision is more determined by when you can go.

In 2011 there are 506 'no fly' cruises leaving and returning to UK ports, of which 85% depart between April and October. But if you are free from time constraints then the longer out of season cruises offer the very best value and some of the world's best cruise itineraries. Imagine leaving from Southampton and experiencing

Amsterdam, Portugal, the Canary Islands, Cape Verde, Brazil, French Guiana, Venezuela, Tobago, Barbados, The Azores and back to Southampton on any other type of holiday, (example itinerary above; Marco Polo's 42 day cruise departing 10th January).

During the cruise season your choice explodes with itineraries from short 3 day taster cruises, through to worldwide explorations.

It is also worth bearing in mind that if you are not travelling with children then it is sensible to investigate the itineraries of adult only ships, especially if you are looking to cruise during the main school holidays.

> *When you can travel will be a decisive factor in where you can travel due to seasonal changes in itineraries.*

Question 2: Where do you want to go?

Firstly, it is worth noting that the new Resort Ships are very much destinations in their own right. The journey is now the holiday and not the destination. Nevertheless, on 'no fly' cruises, whilst you can go just about anywhere, it pretty much boils down to starting out 'north' or 'south'!

Sail north and the Netherlands, Northern France, around UK, Scandinavia, the Norwegian Fjords, the Baltic States, Russia and the Northern Lights are all available as destinations. A short cruise to Amsterdam and back may just be the perfect 'taster' to get you into the maritime mood before taking the plunge into a longer option. The majestic fjords are truly awe-inspiring and never more so than from the prow of a ship. And with the Baltic States and Russia fully open for tourism the jewels of the Tsars are an extraordinary sight.

Many of the cruises have cultural interests and options with museum trips, heritage tours and specialist speakers all available. Whilst the Northern Lights is an experience not to be missed and are best seen towards the end of September when they are most visible.

Sail south for short & medium length cruises to the Mediterranean offering a wealth of alternative itineraries and style of cruises, whilst winter sun seekers can sail down to North Africa and the Canary Islands. For longer durations transatlantic cruises, the Caribbean, South America and Worldwide cruises are all available to the 'no fly' holidaymaker.

Destinations by duration

The maps show the approximate distances you can travel on a 'no fly' cruise, dependent on its duration. As always it is best to talk to your independent 'no fly' cruise specialist who will outline all the options available to you so that you can narrow your choice down to suit your own specific requirements.

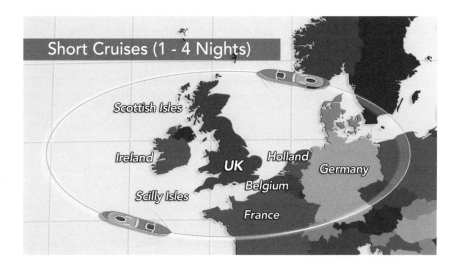

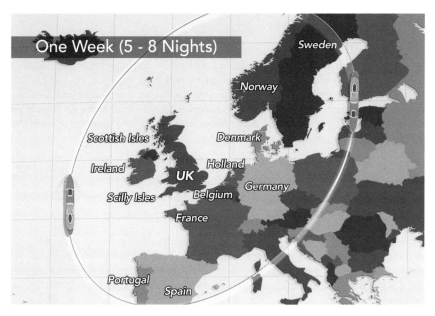

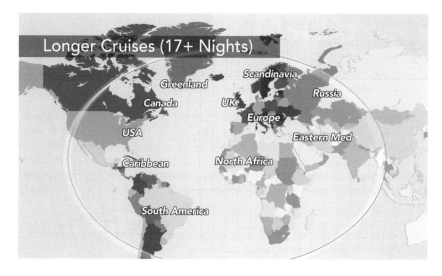

Question 3: How long do you want your 'no fly' cruise to be?

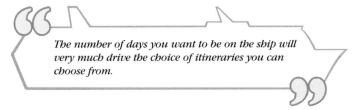

The number of days you want to be on the ship will very much drive the choice of itineraries you can choose from.

This question very much relates to the first two questions in that if you have decided to cruise in January and are looking for sunshine then a short cruise is really out of the question. Naturally if you are working or have children *(or obviously both)* then the duration of the cruise becomes an important consideration in conjunction with where you want to get to.

During the main season *(May-October)* 'no fly' cruises of most durations are available and if this is your most important consideration then this will make your decision making process easier.

The only real advise here is that if you do decide to 'fly cruise' then take into consideration your journey time to and from your country/port of departure/arrival as this can add as much as four days to the length of your holiday spent travelling, over and above the duration of the cruise. Apart from the extra travel time itself, a 'fly cruise' requires extra time allowances in case of unforeseen travel or airport delays - a ship will not hang around for someone stuck at an airport!

Question 4: What style of 'no fly' cruise would best suit you?

In the last ten years the cruise industry has developed so many variations of themed cruises that there is bound to be one that suits you. This growth has been stimulated by requests from passengers wishing to indulge their interests whilst enjoying the overall cruise experience.

So if you're looking for cruises for bridge players, dancers, music or sports lovers, history & world affairs, wellness, political, nature, cultural, lifestyle, food & wine, faith-based and gay & lesbian cruises, these are all available in 2011. However, the nature of special interests means that if this is your primary requirement then you are likely to have to compromise on ship, destination and duration. Our best advice is to talk to your independent 'no fly' cruise specialist as they are best informed to ensure that as many of your pre-requisites are satisfied as possible.

Certain 'no fly' cruise ships do broadly specialise in providing cruises in a certain style and are aimed at specific target audiences.

Suitable for more mature adults

These tend to be the UK based or operated lines that instinctively know what the traditional UK customer is looking for; whether it is formal dress at dinner or simply tea and coffee making facilities in each cabin. So if you are looking for this style of cruise then the following are lines that are most likely to satisfy this preference:

O *Cunard Line*
O *P&O Cruises*
O *Cruise & Maritime*
O *Fred Olsen*
O *Hebridean Island Cruises*
O *Noble Caledonia*
O *Oceania Cruises*
O *Saga Cruises*
O *Swan Hellenic*
O *Voyages of Discovery*

> *When you talk to your 'no fly' cruise specialist make sure that you clearly explain exactly what type of holiday you are looking for so that the right Cruise Line and ship is selected.*

Great for families

This market has seen the largest growth in recent times with many of the mega-ships that have come in to service designed to appeal to a broad age range of families from the very young to the more mature. But do remember, if you are not keen on the noise of 'little distractions' then school holidays are best avoided. Most of the Cruise Lines have certain ships that are better equipped to cater for families. The best ships for families operating in the UK 'no 'fly' market are:

O *Queen Elizabeth, Queen Mary 2 & Queen Victoria with Cunard Line*
O *Eurodam and Ryndam with Holland America Line*
O *Costa Magica with Costa Cruises*
O *Grand Princess & Crown Princess with Princess Cruises*
O *Oriana, Ventura, Oceana, Azura & Aurora with P&O Cruises*
O *Independence of the Seas and Jewel of the Seas with Royal Caribbean International*
O *MSC Opera with MSC Cruises*

Perfect for the less formal cruiser

With the fast growth of cruising as a holiday option this has meant that the style of cruising as a traditional, formal affair has been pretty much relegated to the bin of history. However, certain ships and lines still maintain a more formal charm and so if you are wishing to cruise in a more relaxed carefree environment you should consider the following Cruise Lines:

O *Costa Cruises*
O *P&O Cruises*
O *Princess Cruises*
O *Royal Caribbean International*
O *MSC Cruises*

More suited to singles

Cruising as a single adult can be expensive and lonely, particularly if you choose the wrong ship.

If you are not sharing a cabin, most Cruise Lines will levy a single supplement for cabins with single occupancy. Essentially, if you are looking to cruise alone you have a choice to make. The first is to accept the single occupancy supplement and look for Cruise Lines and ships that generally try to keep these supplements relatively low; for example, Crystal Cruises, Voyages of Discovery or Saga Cruises.

> *Single supplements vary greatly from Cruise Line to Cruise Line so be sure to do your homework before you book.*

Alternatively some Cruise Lines operate Guaranteed Share Programmes where you pay for a cabin in the grade you want on the basis of twin occupancy and the Cruise Line agrees to 'match' you with a companion of the same sex and similar tastes to yourself. The upside is that you will pay a much lower price and may gain a friend for life. Plus, in exceptional circumstances where the Cruise Line is unable to match you up, you may end up in a cabin on your own without having to pay a supplement. On the downside of course is the possibility that you will be stuck with the cabin-mate from hell!

Some Cruise Lines still offer gentleman social hosts for the benefit of single female passengers, whose role is to socialise with single female guests and act as Dance & Bridge partners. If this is what you are looking for then Cunard Line, Crystal Cruises, Holland America Line, Regent Seven Seas Cruises and Silversea Cruises all offer this service.

Picking the right ship

> *Be clear on the type and size of ship you see yourself travelling on. If you're not sure then discuss this with your 'no fly' cruise specialist.*

Large Resort Ships that offer 'no fly' cruising options
(1,600 to 5,000 passengers)

These are called 'resort' ships because that is exactly what they are. They offer the facilities of a land based resort with plenty of activities for children of all ages. If you are looking for a wide variety of food options, state of the art entertainment, smooth sailing in even quite rough seas then these ships are the ideal solution. However, service tends to be 'one size fits all' with additional purchasable extras available for virtually everything. Inevitably with so many people squeeze points can sometimes occur at locations such as buffets, tender launch areas, embarkation and disembarkation.

Ships in this class that offer UK 'no fly' itineraries are:

O *Celebrity Cruises - Celebrity Eclipse*
O *Costa Cruises – Costa Magica*
O *Cunard Line - Queen Elizabeth, Queen Mary 2 & Queen Victoria*
O *Holland America Line - Eurodam*
O *MSC Cruises - MSC Opera*
O *Princess Cruises - Grand Princess & Crown Princess*
O *P&O Cruises - Oriana, Ventura, Oceana, Arcadia, Azura & Aurora*
O *Royal Caribbean International - Independence of the Seas & Jewel of the Seas*

Mid-Size Ships that offer 'no fly' cruising options
(600 to 1,600 passengers)

Mid-Size Ships tend to be a happy medium between those looking for a cruise with some of the advantages of a large resort ship (reasonable stability on rough seas with a good range of facilities, activities, dining options and cabin grades) along with a more personal service that is evident on the smaller ships. Mid-size ships offer a wider range of cruise itineraries and cruise durations as they are equipped for longer / round the world sailings.

Ships in this class that offer UK 'no fly' itineraries are:

O *Classic International - Athena*
O *Cruise & Maritime - Marco Polo & Ocean Countess*
O *Crystal Cruises - Crystal Serenity*
O *Fred Olsen Cruises - Black Watch, Balmoral, Boudica & Braemar*
O *Holland America - Prinsedam & Ryndam*
O *Oceania Cruises - Marina*
O *Princess Cruises - Ocean Princess*
O *P&O Cruises – Artemis & Adonia*
O *Voyages of Discovery - MV Discovery*
O *Regent Seven Seas Cruises - Seven Seas Voyager*
O *Saga Cruises - Saga Pearl II*

Small Ships *(200-600 passengers)* and **Boutique Ships** *(50-200 passengers)* offer more intimate cruises for a smaller number of passengers. Many of the world's most luxurious ships come under this category, but so do many that offer true value for money. They compete against their larger 'sisters' by offering a much more personal and attentive service, akin to the traditional imagery of an ocean-going cruise experience. There is a limit to the size and scale of the entertainment these ships are able to offer and casinos and cinemas are often not available. But, because of their size the quality of their dining experience tends to be first class, queues are rare and they are able to take advantage of smaller ports that the larger ships are unable to dock in.

Ships in this class that offer UK 'no fly' itineraries are:

O *Compagnie du Ponant - Le Diamant (boutique)*
O *Hebridean Cruises - Hebridean Princess (boutique)*
O *Lindblad Expeditions - Lord of the Glens (boutique)*
O *Noble Caledonia - Island Sky (boutique)*
O *Polar Star Expeditions - Polar Star (expedition)*
O *Saga Cruises - Saga Ruby (small)*
O *Silversea Cruises - Silver Cloud (small) & Prince Albert II (boutique)*
O *Swan Hellenic Cruises - Minerva (small)*

Question 5: What's your budget?

The writer Kurt Vonnegut is credited with the quote *'in this world, you get what you pay for'* and this is never truer than with a cruise holiday. There will always be an instance of someone getting the bargain of the century, but for everyone who does, there are hundreds more who have concentrated on the price to the detriment of the value and have ended up with a holiday that was nowhere near as good as their expectation of it.

The chapter later in this book entitled *How to get the best deal on your 'no fly' cruise holiday* explains how the cruise industry prices its cruises, how they are distributed, who sells them and how you can ensure that you get the best price for the cruise you want.

The question here is more related to ensuring that the cruise you choose is exactly right for you. So, be honest, how much do you want to pay?

When discussing your budget with your independent 'no fly' cruise specialist do make sure that you are clear as to exactly what your budget actually covers. They will no doubt talk you through the comparison between a cruise holiday and one in a land based resort or hotel; except that you have probably made the decision to cruise by the time you make this call and so the comparison is pretty irrelevant. More important is the difference in price between a 'no fly' cruise and one in which you join a ship in foreign climes.

Typical Hotel Versus Cruise Holiday Comparison

	European Hotel 14 Nights	Mediterranean Fly Cruise 14 Nights	Mediterranean 'No Fly' Cruise 14 Nights
Base Price*	£700	£1,299	£919
Flight Cost	£160	included	£0
Airport / Port Parking	£112	£112	£105
Car Hire	£360	n/a	n/a
Meals*	£1,050	£0	£0
Tips	£50	£98	£98
Entertainment**	£60	£0	£0
Activites**	£100	£0	£0
Total	£2,592.00	£1,509.00	£1,122.00
Per Day	£185.14	£107.79	£80.14

* The hotel price is based on a 4-Star hotel booked on a B&B basis in Majorca during May 2011 and assumes a budget of £75 per day for lunch and dinner. The Cruise prices are for Mediterranean Cruises taken during May 2011. All prices are correct at time of print (Jan 2011)

** Assumes two theatre / concert tickets + four sporting or leisure activities over the 14 days

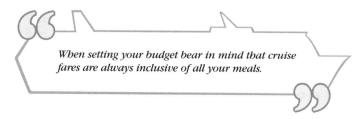

When setting your budget bear in mind that cruise fares are always inclusive of all your meals.

Additional costs to take into consideration

Cruise Lines advertise the fact that 'almost everything's included' but this is rarely the case. Your cruise cost generally covers the ship as transportation, your cabin, meals, entertainment, activities and service on board. So what else do you need to take into consideration?

Cancellation Protection Insurance
It is always sensible to take out cancellation protection insurance. You are generally booking and paying well in advance and you should make sure that you are adequately covered. Do make sure that any forms are completed accurately and that you review the terms of the policies to ensure that they cover exactly what you would expect of them.

Travel Insurance
The best advice here is to shop around and don't routinely take the first insurance that is offered to you. Pay close attention to the terms of the insurance, particularly in the areas of 'pre-existing medical conditions' and the level of cover for lost valuables. When taking out travel insurance make sure that it covers your particular needs and ensure that it is under-written by a reputable company.

Journey costs to port of embarkation
Depending on where you live and your port of embarkation you will need to factor in travel costs; whether it is train, plane, coach tickets or petrol costs.

Parking
Parking at a UK port varies in price depending on port and duration, but as an example Harwich daily parking cost is £7.50 and Southampton is approximately £10 per day.

Laundry
On longer cruises you are likely to want to avail yourself of the laundry facilities, particularly on more traditional ships where formal dress is expected in the dining room. The Cruise Lines' brochures will all indicate that laundry services are available for a nominal charge, but even nominal charges can add up, so do take this into consideration.

Little extras
These can cover everything from a few ice creams to spa treatments, the ship photographer, wine tasting, internet access, telephone calls and other specialist activities. Remember, a cruise ship is a business and just as a cinema will endeavour to sell you popcorn and soft drinks, so a cruise ship will focus on selling any number of optional extras. But they are optional, so if something is important to you then budget for it.

Medical Services
All ships will have a qualified Doctor on board, but these are normally operated as a concession and so charges will apply. Many insurance packages will cover medical requirements, so make sure yours does should the eventuality arise.

> *Generally all UK ports include transportation from your car park to the ship and that includes arrangements to get your luggage to the ship.*

Port Taxes
These are levied by individual port authorities and are usually shown in the brochure. They are normally charged as part of your cruise cost, but do make sure that you check this.

Fuel surcharges
All Cruise Lines have a clause in their terms and conditions that allow them to levy a fuel surcharge on top of the cruise fare should fuel costs rise between the date of booking and cruise departure.

Drinks
On a cruise you are a captive market and so drinks costs, even for soft drinks and bottled water, can mount up. Your independent 'no fly' cruise specialist can give you an indication as to costs, but it is better to over budget than to be surprised on your last night.

> *Drinks are a major source of revenue for Cruise Lines and they will be pushing drinks onto you at every opportunity. Make sure you always ask the cost and then decide whether you want to proceed.*

Shore excursions

Almost all shore excursions are an additional cost, unless you are on an adventure or expedition cruise where they tend to be included as they form an integral part of the cruises experience. Most Cruise Lines now offer you the opportunity to buy your excursions in advance of your cruise, which can often save you time and sometimes money. However, do be aware that on a cruise your priorities do change and what was previously a great excursion can be usurped by another or even the desire to stay onboard ship. In these instances the Cruise Lines' cancellation and refund policies come into effect and as a general rule they tend to be pretty strict.

Even if you choose not to purchase your excursions in advance do read the information online or discuss with your independent 'no fly' cruise specialist and make some early decisions as to which appeal to you. Queues for shore excursion tickets can get quite long, particularly on large ships and on the first few days of a cruise.

> *Shore excursions purchased onboard are often considerably more expensive than can be purchased pier-side for the same tour.*

Gratuities

Tipping is a fact of life at the end of a cruise and most Cruise Lines now publish a recommended tipping guide to avoid confusion or embarrassment. Some will also include a sum on your final bill, but remember you are entitled to decrease or increase this recommendation dependent on the quality of service you received. As a rule of thumb you are expected to tip your Dining Room Waiter, Assistant Waiter and Cabin Steward on the last night of your cruise and you should budget approximately £4-£7 per day.

Gratuities by Cruise Line

Line	Are Tips Expected?	Adult Daily Rate	Children Daily Rate	Additional Charges
Celebrity Cruises	Yes	$11.50-$15	$11.50-$15	15% on Drinks and beauty treatments
Classic International Cruises	No	N/A	N/A	None
Compagnie du Ponant	Yes	12E	12E	None
Costa Cruises	Yes	7E-11E	Under 14 None	15% on Drinks and beauty treatments
Cruise and Maritime Voyages	Yes	£4-£5	None	None
Crystal Cruises	Yes	$13	$13	15% on Drinks and beauty treatments
Cunard Cruises	Yes	$11-$13	$11-$13	15% on Drinks and beauty treatments
Fred Olsen Cruise Line	Yes	£4	N/A	None
Hebridean Island Cruises	No	N/A	N/A	None
Holland America Line	Yes	$11	$11	15% on Drinks
Lindblad Expeditions	Yes	£4-£5	N/A	None
MSC Cruises	Yes	£6-£12	Under 14 None	15% on Drinks
Noble Caledonia	Yes	£5-£10	N/A	Varies on each vessel
Oceania Cruises	Yes	$12.50-$16.50	$12.50-$16.50	18% on Drinks and beauty treatments
P & O Cruises	Yes	£6-£12	Under 12 None	None
Princess Cruises	Yes	$10.50-$11	$10.50-$11	15% on Drinks and beauty treatments
Regent Seven Seas Cruises	No	Included	Included	Included
Royal Caribbean Cruises	Yes	$9.75-$12	$9.75-$12	10-15% on Drinks
Silversea	No	Included	Included	Included
Swan Hellenic	No	N/A	N/A	Beauty Treatments only
Voyages of Discovery	No	N/A	N/A	None

The above information is shown as a guide only. Please check with the individual Cruise Lines or your 'no fly' cruise specialist before booking a cruise.
E = Euros
$ = US Dollars

The main 'no fly' Cruise Lines & ships

CELEBRITY CRUISES

Celebrity Cruises operates 11 ships across the 7-seas. One of their vessels, the Celebrity Eclipse, is deployed in the 'no fly' market departing from Southampton during the summer.

The Celebrity Eclipse offers a couple of short taster cruises to Cork in the spring and several 14 night cruises that visit some of the most attractive ports in the Mediterranean, Scandinavia & Russia. The product appeals to passengers who are looking for an understated luxury holiday, outstanding cuisine and excellent ship entertainment, without breaking the bank. As a consequence Celebrity offers some of the best value in the cruise industry today and is popular with the British market. The language on board is English so the entire product is very much suited to the British cruiser.

The Celebrity Eclipse is suited to all customers but in particular to families with older children and teenagers.

On a Celebrity Cruise staterooms and suites blend old-world elegance with state-of-the-art technology. The latest therapies and treatments are available in the luxurious Aqua Spa, and in the dining room the service is matched with the world-renowned cuisine of Master Chef Michel Roux. Expect to be pampered and entertained on board one of the youngest and most sophisticated ships on the seas today.

The Celebrity Eclipse's stated goal is to exceed all expectations and despite the ship's 4 Star Plus rating the cruise fares remain extremely competitive and in line with other moderately priced products in this category. The style and size of the ship is appealing to the family and mature adult markets alike.

CELEBRITY CRUISES

Ship Offering
No Fly Itineraries   **Celebrity Eclipse**

Built	2010
Latest Refit	nil
Rating	4-star Plus
Category	Large Resort
Recommended For	Families
Price Point	Premium
Currency on Board	USD
Tonnage	122,000
Total Cabins	1,425
Inside	210
Outside	58
Balcony	1,157
Total Berths	3,145
Family Friendly?	yes
Kids Club	yes
Passenger Decks	14
Wheelchair Cabins	26
Elevators	10
Dining Options	Two Sittings
Casino	yes
Show Lounge	yes
Fitness Centre	yes
Swimming Pool (internal)	1
Swimming Pool (external)	2
Self Service Laundrette	no
Cinema	no
Library	yes
Cabin Current	110 & 220 Volts
Wi-Fi	yes

CLASSIC INTERNATIONAL CRUISES

Classic International Cruises provide excellent value cruising on Portuguese run older classic liners. The atmosphere onboard is casual and homely, but without the facilities of the newer ships. What these ships lack in facilities is very much made up by the excellent and attentive service onboard; staff are friendly, have a great knack of remembering your names and as such cannot do enough to ensure the cruise experience is not only top class, but also memorable.

The cuisine onboard is very international and has a Portuguese influence serving lots of fish and meat dishes. Cabin choice is restricted to inside and ocean view cabins with no balcony cabins being available. The product attracts mainly mature couples as there are no children's facilities available and hence deemed unsuitable for the family market. Classic International Cruises operate some more specialised itineraries as they are able to visit many ports whose infrastructure is unable to accommodate the larger vessels.

One of their 3 ships the **Athena** is deployed from the UK in the spring from Dover, Rosyth and Newcastle and 3 cruises *(during 2011)* are available for the 'no fly' market. The cruises are targeted at mature passengers looking for a value for money traditional cruise experience aboard a classic liner.

COMPAGNIE DU PONANT

Compagnie du Ponant only offers one 'no fly' cruise aboard their small boutique ship **Le Diamant** departing from Portsmouth in July. The 7 Night cruise visits ports in Ireland, Wales, St. Malo in France before returning to Portsmouth. The ship will appeal to passengers looking for an upscale cruise experience aboard a boutique ship.

On your cruise, you will find there is plenty to do. You can tend to your body and get yourself in shape with expert guidance of a fitness trainer. There are regular nautical activities on the agenda: wind-surfing, water-skiing and diving. But if you just want to take a break, then you can settle down on a deck and revel in doing nothing.

CLASSIC INTERNATIONAL CRUISES

Ship Offering No Fly Itineraries	Athena
Built	1948
Latest Refit	2004
Rating	2-Star
Category	Small
Recommended For	Mature Couples
Price Point	Economy
Currency on Board	GBP
Tonnage	16,144
Total Cabins	276
Inside	48
Outside	220
Balcony	8
Total Berths	641
Family Friendly?	Unsuitable
Kids Club	no
Passenger Decks	7
Wheelchair Cabins	0
Elevators	2
Dining Options	Two Sittings
Casino	yes
Show Lounge	yes
Fitness Centre	yes
Swimming Pool (internal)	0
Swimming Pool (external)	1
Self Service Laundrette	no
Cinema	no
Library	yes
Cabin Current	220 volts
Wi-Fi	no

COMPAGNIE DU PONANT

Ship Offering No Fly Itineraries	Le Diamant
Built	1986
Latest Refit	1990
Rating	4-Star
Category	Small Boutique
Recommended For	Mature Couples
Price Point	Luxury
Currency on Board	EURO
Tonnage	8,282
Total Cabins	113
Inside	0
Outside	103
Balcony	10
Total Berths	226
Family Friendly?	Unsuitable
Kids Club	no
Passenger Decks	6
Wheelchair Cabins	0
Elevators	2
Dining Options	One Sitting
Casino	yes
Show Lounge	yes
Fitness Centre	yes
Swimming Pool (internal)	0
Swimming Pool (external)	1
Self Service Laundrette	no
Cinema	no
Library	yes
Cabin Current	220 volts
Wi-Fi	yes

COSTA CRUISES

Costa Cruises operate 15 ships which are mostly deployed in the Mediterranean during the summer and then repositioned to other parts of the globe during the winter.

One of their ships, the **Costa Magica**, is deployed from both Dover & Harwich during the summer for the 'no fly' cruising market, mainly to Scandinavia & Russia. The cruises are generally 10 nights in duration.

The Costa Magica is a large resort ship ideally suited to the family market, offering great facilities for children; a kid's club, kid's pool, arcade as well as plenty of outdoor spaces on the decks for an enjoyable break whilst at sea. The Costa Magica, due to her size, offers varied dining options, excellent nightly theatre entertainment and plenty happening out on the open decks. If you are looking for a cruise slightly longer than a week then the Costa Magica is certainly an option worth considering.

Whichever Costa cruise you choose, one thing is guaranteed – you'll enjoy a unique level of hospitality for which Costa has become renowned. Think of Italy and you'll imagine modern design, fine style, first-class cuisine and warm hospitality – and these are some of the ingredients that make Costa Cruises unique. On the back of the exceptional service, outstanding value for money and high level of repeat business, Costa has grown to now be the largest Cruise Line in Europe.

CRUISE & MARITIME VOYAGES

Marco Polo and **Ocean Countess** are operated under charter by Cruise & Maritime Voyages who have a wealth of cruise industry expertise spanning almost four decades and are members of the prestigious Passenger Shipping Association and ACE – the Association of Cruise Experts.

For many years Cruise & Maritime Voyages have specialised in providing 'no fly' cruising holidays aboard small and medium sized classic and more traditional style ships. They believe these vessels, which are generally owned by independent and privately owned shipping companies, offer a more leisurely and friendly 'home from home' style of cruising and are accessible to a much wider choice of interesting and remote ports of call.

The 'no fly' cruises offered by Cruises & Maritime range from 3 to 16 nights in duration and cover destinations such as the Canaries, the Scandinavian Fjords & Russian Capitals, the British Isles and much more. Cruise & Maritime Voyages offer the most departure ports in the UK with cruises available from Hull, Tilbury, Newcastle, Liverpool, Dublin, Falmouth and Edinburgh and so not only suit the 'no fly' market well, but also caters for those cruisers who are looking to find cruises departing from ports much closer to home.

COSTA CRUISES

Ship Offering No Fly Itineraries	Costa Magica
Built	2004
Latest Refit	nil
Rating	4-Star
Category	Large Resort
Recommended For	Families
Price Point	Moderate
Currency on Board	EURO
Tonnage	105,000
Total Cabins	1,358
Inside	212
Outside	324
Balcony	522
Total Berths	3,470
Family Friendly?	yes
Kids Club	yes
Passenger Decks	13
Wheelchair Cabins	14
Elevators	14
Dining Options	Two Sittings
Casino	yes
Show Lounge	yes
Fitness Centre	yes
Swimming Pool (internal)	0
Swimming Pool (external)	3
Self Service Laundrette	no
Cinema	no
Library	yes
Cabin Current	220 volts
Wi-Fi	yes

CRUISE & MARITIME VOYAGES

Ship Offering No Fly Itineraries	Marco Polo	Ocean Countess
Built	1966	1976
Latest Refit	1993	2006
Rating	3-Star	3-Star
Category	Small	Small
Recommended For	Mature Couples	Mature Couples
Price Point	Economy	Economy
Currency on Board	GBP	GBP
Tonnage	22,080	17,593
Total Cabins	425	400
Inside	131	135
Outside	294	265
Balcony	0	0
Total Berths	800	800
Family Friendly?	Unsuitable	Unsuitable
Kids Club	no	no
Passenger Decks	8	8
Wheelchair Cabins	2	2
Elevators	4	2
Dining Options	Two Sittings	Two Sittings
Casino	no	yes
Show Lounge	yes	yes
Fitness Centre	yes	yes
Swimming Pool (internal)	0	0
Swimming Pool (external)	1	1
Self Service Laundrette	no	no
Cinema	no	yes
Library	yes	yes
Cabin Current	110 & 220 volts	110 & 220 volts
Wi-Fi	no	no

CRYSTAL CRUISES

Crystal Cruises epitomises luxury wherever you look. One cruise is available to the 'no fly' market during 2011 aboard the 6-Star *Crystal Serenity* departing from Dover in July. As the only Crystal cruise which operates on a 'no fly' basis this summer it is bound to be popular with passengers looking for an ultra luxury cruise experience that does not require the inconvenience of airports and flights to reach your ship.

Luxury as they say is in the details and it is so often the little details that make the difference. From the moment you step aboard a Crystal Ship you will experience their dedication to making your cruise absolutely perfect. Crystal is committed to ensuring your cruise is memorable; from the grand designs of their ship to the right vintage wine, a turned down bed, singular attention is paid to every detail of your cruise. For Crystal quality means the constant pursuit of a single goal and that is to create the best and then make it better.

Their chefs prepare the finest cuisine from around the world, the dining experience very much reflects the service in each of the dining rooms and the entire experience is generally far more formal than on other ships; smart casual clothing during the day, jackets and ties for the gents in the evenings.

This Japanese owned, but American marketed line, provides cruisers with a deluxe experience.

REGENT SEVEN SEAS CRUISES

Regent Seven Seas operates one cruise during the mid summer around the British Isles in the 'no fly' category onboard the *Seven Seas Voyager*. The Cruise Line and this itinerary very much target's the 6 star passenger who is seeking one of the finest Cruise Lines in the world. If nothing but the best will do then the Seven Seas Voyager is certainly a product worth considering.

Regent Seven Seas Cruises offer luxury vessels which are designed for guests numbering in the hundreds rather than the thousands. The ambiance on board is personal, individual and accommodating. All their ships share certain similarities in the quality of their cabins, service, dining and amenities that elevate them to six star status.

CRYSTAL CRUISES

Ship Offering No Fly Itineraries	Crystal Serenity
Built	2003
Latest Refit	nil
Rating	6-Star
Category	Medium Resort
Recommended For	Mature Couples
Price Point	Ultra Luxury
Currency on Board	USD
Tonnage	68,000
Total Cabins	548
Inside	0
Outside	81
Balcony	464
Total Berths	1,080
Family Friendly?	Acceptable
Kids Club	no
Passenger Decks	9
Wheelchair Cabins	8
Elevators	8
Dining Options	Two Sittings
Casino	yes
Show Lounge	yes
Fitness Centre	yes
Swimming Pool (internal)	1
Swimming Pool (external)	1
Self Service Laundrette	yes
Cinema	yes
Library	yes
Cabin Current	110 & 220 volts
Wi-Fi	yes

REGENT SEVEN SEAS

Ship Offering No Fly Itineraries	Seven Seas Voyager
Built	2003
Latest Refit	2009
Rating	6-Star
Category	Mid-Size
Recommended For	Mature Couples
Price Point	Ultra Luxury
Currency on Board	USD
Tonnage	50,000
Total Cabins	354
Inside	0
Outside	0
Balcony	354
Total Berths	752
Family Friendly?	Unsuitable
Kids Club	no
Passenger Decks	9
Wheelchair Cabins	6
Elevators	5
Dining Options	Open Dining
Casino	yes
Show Lounge	yes
Fitness Centre	yes
Swimming Pool (internal)	0
Swimming Pool (external)	1
Self Service Laundrette	yes
Cinema	no
Library	yes
Cabin Current	110 volts
Wi-Fi	yes

CUNARD LINE

The Cunard Line operates three vessels in the luxury market; *Queen Mary 2, Queen Victoria* and the brand new *Queen Elizabeth* which only entered service in late 2010.

All three ships offer 'no fly' cruise itineraries at various times of the year which range from the Canaries or Scandinavia & Russia to a full circumnavigation of the globe. They also offer a couple of short sampler cruises that may well whet your appetite for some of their longer and exciting itineraries.

For holidaymakers who are reluctant to fly there is ample choice in itineraries from 5 to 103 days to choose from. The Cunard ships appeal to passengers who are looking for a traditional British experience; understated luxury, outstanding cuisine & white glove service in the dining room with a slightly more formal dress code. Gala entertainment is provided nightly in the theatre and there is plenty to do to keep you busy all day long.

Cunard generally appeals more to the mature adult market but the range of their children's clubs and facilities offers the family market a great cruise, regardless of which ship you choose.

So pick your passion, whether it is the unique tradition of an ocean liner crossing, or a majestic cruise to a fascinating locale. The Cunard itineraries blend the best of the past with a vision of the future. You can retrace the routes of the Cape Town liners, worship the sun and gaze at the stars on leisurely Southern Crossings or discover the pleasures of a more cultured itinerary.

Cunard is the only Cruise Line today which allocates the dining room for the entire cruise on the basis of category of cabin purchased. All restaurants represent a 5-star dining experience for each of your meals and irrespective of the restaurant assigned all facilities and entertainment offered on each voyage is available to all guests and are not linked to the type of cabin purchased.

CUNARD LINE

Ship Offering No Fly Itineraries	Queen Elizabeth	Queen Mary 2	Queen Victoria
Built	2010	2003	2007
Latest Refit	nil	nil	
Rating	5-star	5 star	5 Star
Category	Large Resort	Large Resort	Large Resort
Recommended For	Adults	Adults	Adults
Price Point	Luxury	Luxury	Luxury
Currency on Board	GBP	GBP	GBP
Tonnage	90,900	148,528	90,000
Total Cabins	1,007	1,320	1,007
Inside	146	265	146
Outside	146	60	146
Balcony	715	995	715
Total Berths	2,172	3,090	2,172
Family Friendly?	yes	yes	yes
Kids Club	yes	yes	yes
Passenger Decks	12	12	12
Wheelchair Cabins	18	30	18
Elevators	18	18	18
Dining Options	Two Sittings	Two Sittings	Two Sittings
Casino	yes	yes	yes
Show Lounge	Yes	Yes	Yes
Fitness Centre	yes	yes	yes
Swimming Pool (internal)	1	2	0
Swimming Pool (external)	2	3	2
Self Service Laundrette	yes	yes	yes
Cinema	no	yes	no
Library	yes	yes	yes
Cabin Current	110 & 220 Volts	110 & 220 Volts	110 & 220 Volts
Wi-Fi	yes	yes	yes

FRED. OLSEN CRUISE LINES

Fred Olsen Cruise Lines is a traditional British operator that very much focuses on the 'no fly' cruise market by possibly offering the widest choice of itineraries in the 'no fly' category. They additionally offer one of the widest choice of UK ports to depart from which include Dover, Rosyth, Portsmouth, Liverpool, Newcastle, Southampton & Greenock (Glasgow). The wide choice means that getting to the nearest port could not get any easier.

The choice of itineraries which include Portugal & the Canaries, Scandinavia, Greenland & Iceland and even longer itineraries, is vast and they certainly offer the cruiser a wide array of options from 7 to 23 nights in duration. If circumnavigation of the globe or a comprehensive visit to South America or the Caribbean holds your interest then this is certainly possible with Fred Olsen and itineraries from 35 nights to 108 nights are packed with the opportunity to visit some of the most exotic ports in the world.

Fred Olsen Cruise Lines has defined and refined the cruise experience, and judging by the extremely high numbers of passengers coming back time and again the Cruise Line seems to have styled the product to match their customers.

Fred Olsen's *Braemar, Black Watch, Boudicca* and the *Balmoral* are small to medium sized ships and as such their emphasis is on you as a welcome guest and not just a cabin number.

Cuisine is traditional, very much designed around the British passenger and is consistently good. Fred Olsen very much targets the mature traveller and the product is deemed unsuitable for families as no children's facilities are offered.

FRED. OLSEN CRUISE LINES

Ship Offering No Fly Itineraries	Balmoral	Black Watch	Boudicca	Braemar
Built	1988	1972	1973	1993
Latest Refit	2008	2009	2006	2008
Rating	4-Star	4-Star	4-Star	4-star
Category	Mid-Size	Small	Small	Small
Recommended For	Mature Couples	Mature Couples	Mature Couples	Mature Couples
Price Point	Moderate	Moderate	Moderate	Moderate
Currency on Board	GBP	GBP	GBP	GBP
Tonnage	43,537	28,613	28,388	24,344
Total Cabins	738	421	437	510
Inside	113	48	64	132
Outside	504	306	308	298
Balcony	121	67	65	80
Total Berths	1,400	868	900	1,075
Family Friendly?	Unsuitable	Unsuitable	Unsuitable	Unsuitable
Kids Club	no	no	no	Limited
Passenger Decks	10	8	8	7
Wheelchair Cabins	9	4	4	4
Elevators	4	5	5	4
Dining Options	Two Sittings	Two Sittings	Two Sittings	Two Sittings
Casino	yes	yes	yes	no
Show Lounge	yes	yes	yes	yes
Fitness Centre	yes	yes	yes	yes
Swimming Pool (internal)	0	0	0	0
Swimming Pool (external)	2	2	2	2
Self Service Laundrette	yes	yes	yes	yes
Cinema	no	yes	no	no
Library	yes	yes	yes	yes
Cabin Current	110 & 220 volts	110 & 220 volts	110& 220 volts	110&220 volts
Wi-Fi	yes	yes	yes	yes

HOLLAND AMERICA LINE

The Holland America Line deploys three of their 15 ships in the UK 'no fly' market; the **Eurodam, Prinsedam** and **Ryndam**.

The children's facilities available onboard the Eurodam and Ryndam, particularly during family holidays, make these ships an excellent choice in the premium family market sector.

The Prinsedam is geared to the more mature traveller looking for a traditional yet upscale cruise option.

Their ships are deployed mainly from Dover and Tilbury visiting many ports in Scandinavia and Russia and additionally operate a couple of Gaelic itineraries. This product is very much favoured by an experienced traveller looking for a quality cruise experience, comfortable accommodation, great cuisine and excellent service in a 5-star environment. Holland America cruises offer excellent value in the moderate luxury market.

HOLLAND AMERICA LINE

Ship Offering No Fly Itineraries	Eurodam	Prinsedam	Ryndam
Built	2008	1988	1994
Latest Refit	nil	1999	nil
Rating	5-Star	5-Star	5-star
Category	Large Resort	Mid-Size	Mid-Size
Recommended For	Families	Mature Couples	Families
Price Point	Premium	Premium	Premium
Currency on Board	USD	USD	USD
Tonnage	86,000	37,845	55,541
Total Cabins	1,022	398	633
Inside	145	27	132
Outside	193	214	352
Balcony	684	147	149
Total Berths	2,250	814	1,627
Family Friendly?	yes	no	yes
Kids Club	yes	no	yes
Passenger Decks	12	9	10
Wheelchair Cabins	21	8	6
Elevators	14	4	8
Dining Options	Two Sittings	Two Sittings	Two Sittings
Casino	yes	yes	yes
Show Lounge	yes	yes	yes
Fitness Centre	yes	yes	yes
Swimming Pool (internal)	2	0	1
Swimming Pool (external)	1	2	1
Self Service Laundrette	no	yes	yes
Cinema	yes	yes	yes
Library	yes	yes	yes
Cabin Current	110 & 220 volts	110 volts	110 & 220 volts
Wi-Fi	yes	yes	yes

HEBRIDEAN ISLAND CRUISES

Hebridean Island Cruises is a British operator offering cruises in Northern European (*mainly Scottish*) waters for those who like the outdoor life, lots of scenery and luxurious accommodation. Informal talks, lectures and social ambiance are key parts of the cruise experience offered.

The **Hebridean Princess**, the flag ship of Hebridean Island Cruises offers 35 cruise departures for 'no fly' passengers. Due to the size of the ship it is not suitable for families as there are no facilities offered for children on board. Their itineraries very much focus on discovering some of the best of Britain visiting some of the famous gardens and castles in many of the British coastal communities.

This ship will appeal to passengers who are looking for a very intimate cruise experience to some of the prettiest destinations Britain has on offer.

With a maximum of only 49 passengers when full, Hebridean is clearly not a cheap mass market offering, but is renowned for a personal level of service which the larger ships cannot practically offer, so if it's ultra-personalised service you are after then Hebridean will not disappoint on this front.

MSC CRUISES

The Mediterranean Shipping Company (*MSC*) owns and operates 11 ships mainly in the mid-size to large resort ship categories.

The company operates one of their mid size ships, the **MSC Opera**, from Southampton during the summer and offers 8 & 10 night itineraries to Scandinavia & Russia.

There is a supervised children's club on board and therefore the ship rates very highly in the family market. The MSC Opera offers an Italian experience with a varied Mediterranean-influenced cuisine, good entertainment in the lounges and outdoor deck areas and most importantly provides the opportunity to visit some of the most popular ports in Northern Europe.

MSC Cruises combines a deep heritage at sea with an enthusiastic, young and motivated management team. They uniquely blend maritime traditions, culture and famous Mediterranean cuisine to deliver a great cruise experience while displaying a real commitment to the finest hospitality afloat. In essence, MSC Cruises has made true Italian service the heart of its business and its key point of differentiation in the cruise industry.

HEBRIDEAN ISLAND CRUISES

Ship Offering No Fly Itineraries	Hebridean Princess
Built	1964
Latest Refit	1989
Rating	5-Star
Category	Small Boutique
Recommended For	Mature Couples
Price Point	Luxury
Currency on Board	GBP
Tonnage	2,112
Total Cabins	30
Inside	6
Outside	20
Balcony	4
Total Berths	49
Family Friendly?	Unsuitable
Kids Club	no
Passenger Decks	5
Wheelchair Cabins	0
Elevators	0
Dining Options	One Sitting
Casino	no
Show Lounge	nil
Fitness Centre	yes
Swimming Pool (internal)	0
Swimming Pool (external)	0
Self Service Laundrette	no
Cinema	no
Library	yes
Cabin Current	240 volts
Wi-Fi	no

MSC CRUISES

Ship Offering No Fly Itineraries	MSC Opera
Built	2003
Latest Refit	nil
Rating	4-Star
Category	Mid-Size
Recommended For	Families
Price Point	Moderate
Currency on Board	EURO
Tonnage	58,600
Total Cabins	856
Inside	354
Outside	297
Balcony	200
Total Berths	2,055
Family Friendly?	yes
Kids Club	yes
Passenger Decks	10
Wheelchair Cabins	5
Elevators	9
Dining Options	Two Sittings
Casino	yes
Show Lounge	yes
Fitness Centre	yes
Swimming Pool (internal)	0
Swimming Pool (external)	2
Self Service Laundrette	no
Cinema	no
Library	yes
Cabin Current	110 & 220 volts
Wi-Fi	yes

NOBLE CALEDONIA

Some years ago, Noble Caledonia detected a need by seasoned travellers for a company that could offer a range of trips that were educational, enjoyable and above all, different. Established in 1991, the company has aimed to provide clients with a lasting memory of a journey made with like-minded travellers. Noble Caledonia continues to expand its repertoire to include new destinations.

Noble Caledonia operates their small 57 cabin ship the *Island Sky* from Portsmouth and Edinburgh. Due to the size of the ship the Island Sky visits some of the prettiest ports that are not possible to reach with larger ships. The ship appeals to clients who prefer a more traditional feel and service offered by a small boutique ship.

OCEANIA CRUISES

Oceania Cruises will deploy their largest ship the *Marina* on a couple of 'no fly' cruises departing from Dover in the heart of summer. The Marina only comes online in early 2011 and it will be the newest ship to enter the 'no fly' cruise category.

Oceania Cruises, despite only having been launched in 2002, has quickly established themselves as a significant player in the 5-Star market. Carrying in excess of 1,200 guests The Marina is no doubt going to be one of the most popular options in this category on the basis that she is so new and frequent cruisers and the Cruise Line's past guests will want to experience this new ship in their home waters. The ship will appeal to passengers who seek a 5-Star product, as the Cruise Line has won many awards in this category, will deliver an understated luxury, offer tremendous cuisine and very high standard of accommodation in their mainly outside & balcony staterooms and suites.

Aboard the Marina the promise is that you will be surrounded by an elegance and level of sophistication reminiscent of an upscale private country club – yours to enjoy in a relaxed, comfortable and unpretentious manner that is never stuffy and void of formality – we look forward to hearing from the first passengers to see whether Oceania have been able to live up to their aspirations.

NOBLE CALEDONIA CRUISES

Ship Offering No Fly Itineraries	Island Sky
Built	1992
Latest Refit	2003
Rating	4-Star
Category	Small Boutique
Recommended For	Mature Couples
Price Point	Moderate
Currency on Board	GBP
Tonnage	4,280
Total Cabins	57
Inside	0
Outside	45
Balcony	12
Total Berths	116
Family Friendly?	Unsuitable
Kids Club	no
Passenger Decks	5
Wheelchair Cabins	0
Elevators	1
Dining Options	One Sitting
Casino	no
Show Lounge	yes
Fitness Centre	yes
Swimming Pool (internal)	0
Swimming Pool (external)	1
Self Service Laundrette	no
Cinema	no
Library	yes
Cabin Current	110 volts
Wi-Fi	yes

OCEANIA CRUISES

Ship Offering No Fly Itineraries	Marina
Built	2011
Latest Refit	nil
Rating	5-Star
Category	Mid-Size
Recommended For	Mature Couples
Price Point	Luxury
Currency on Board	USD
Tonnage	66,000
Total Cabins	629
Inside	18
Outside	20
Balcony	591
Total Berths	1,258
Family Friendly?	Unsuitable
Kids Club	no
Passenger Decks	11
Wheelchair Cabins	3
Elevators	6
Dining Options	Open Dining
Casino	yes
Show Lounge	yes
Fitness Centre	yes
Swimming Pool (internal)	0
Swimming Pool (external)	1
Self Service Laundrette	yes
Cinema	no
Library	yes
Cabin Current	110 & 220 volts
Wi-Fi	yes

P & O CRUISES

P&O Cruises is possibly the best known cruise brand in the UK market and offers in excess of 25% of all the available capacity in the 'no fly' cruise category. The overall majority of ships on offer are well suited to both the family and adult markets, with their adult only ships the *Arcadia, Artemis* and the *Adonia* providing the mature British traveller with a choice of vessels they can travel on. P&O offers a wide choice of cruise itineraries ranging from 3 night taster cruises to 98 night around the world cruises. All P&O cruises depart from their home port of Southampton.

P&O have been perfecting the art of cruising for over 170 years and that experience provides them with unrivalled knowledge of the world and all that it has to offer. A

Ship Offering No Fly Itineraries	Adonia	Arcadia	Artemis
Built	2001	2004	1984
Latest Refit	2007	2008	2005
Rating	4- star	4-star	4-star
Category	Mid -Size	Large Resort	Mid -Size
Recommended For	Adults	Adults	Adults
Price Point	Moderate	Moderate	Moderate
Currency on Board	GBP	GBP	GBP
Tonnage	30,277	82,972	45,000
Total Cabins	335	984	530
Inside	26	136	0
Outside	77	174	443
Balcony	232	708	146
Total Berths	838	2,456	1,260
Family Friendly?	no	no	no
Kids Club	no	no	no
Passenger Decks	9	10	9
Wheelchair Cabins	3	18	4
Elevators	4	14	6
Dining Options	Two Sittings	Two Sittings	Two Sittings
Casino	yes	yes	yes
Show Lounge	yes	yes	yes
Fitness Centre	yes	yes	yes
Swimming Pool (internal)	0	0	0
Swimming Pool (external)	1	2	2
Self Service Laundrette	yes	yes	yes
Cinema	no	yes	yes
Library	yes	yes	yes
Cabin Current	110& 220Volts	110& 220 volts	110 & 220volts
Wi-Fi	yes	yes	yes

NoFlyCruising.com

P&O Cruise holiday offers exceptional value and is tailored specifically for British passengers, whilst encompassing a wide selection of destinations and durations.

You can expect friendly service and sophisticated surroundings whichever ship you choose, with each providing everything from West End style entertainment, Michelin starred chefs, silver service dining and classic afternoon tea, to home comforts such as tea and coffee making facilities in your cabin. Sterling is the standard currency on board and English spoken throughout.

The ships targeted towards a broad family market include the *Aurora, Oceana, Oriana* and the two largest ships in their fleet, the *Ventura* and *Azura*. All offer a wide variety of children's facilities and activities on board.

Aurora	Azura	Oceana	Oriana	Ventura
2000	2010	2000	1995	2008
nil	nil	2002	nil	nil
4-Star	4-Star	4-Star	4-Star	4-Star
Large Resort	Large Resort	Large Resort	Large Resort	Large Resort
Families	Families	Families	Families	Families
Moderate	Moderate	Moderate	Moderate	Moderate
GBP	GBP	GBP	GBP	GBP
76,000	116,000	77,000	69,000	116,000
939	1,532	1,008	911	1,532
284	433	405	319	433
245	227	193	474	227
410	872	410	118	872
1,950	3,100	2,272	1,928	3,574
yes	yes	yes	yes	yes
yes	yes	yes	yes	yes
10	14	10	10	15
22	32	19	8	32
10	16	11	10	16
Two Sittings	Two Sittings	Two Sittings	Two Sittings	Two Sittings
yes	yes	yes	yes	yes
yes	yes	yes	yes	yes
yes	yes	yes	yes	yes
1	0	0	0	2
3	3	4	3	3
yes	yes	yes	yes	yes
yes	no	no	yes	no
yes	yes	yes	yes	yes
110 & 220 volts	110 & 220 volts	110 & 220 volts	110 &220 Volts	220 volts
yes	yes	yes	yes	yes

POLAR STAR EXPEDITIONS

Polar Star Expeditions targets the cruise expedition market. The *Polar Star* is an infrequent visitor to our shores and is only scheduled to perform one cruise in May around the Scottish coastline and islands. The ship is small, with only 45 cabins, and can therefore dock in some of the smallest ports and visit the smallest communities.

The Polar Star is the expedition cruising vessel of Polar Star Expeditions. The company is headquartered in Halifax, Canada and is a Norwegian Company owned by Karlsen Shipping Company which was founded in Norway more than 100 years ago.

Polar Star Expeditions has a mission "to create meaningful and memorable cruise expeditions to remote destinations – alive with the energy and power of untouched nature".

LINDBLAD EXPEDITIONS

This is strictly an expedition product that appeals to clients looking for a slightly off the beaten track experience. *The Lord of the Glens*, their expedition vessel, departs from Inverness and offers four 'no fly' cruises in 2011, with itineraries around the Scottish Isles. With only 27 cabins on the ship these cruises will certainly require early booking.

Linblad take small groups of adventurous travellers to out-of-the-way places on nimble expedition ships that nose into ports and call on islands where larger cruise ships simply cannot go. Expedition leaders and naturalists onboard are experts in their field with a passion for uncovering and interpreting the mysteries of nature and history.

POLAR STAR EXPEDITIONS

Ship Offering No Fly Itineraries	Polar Star
Built	1966
Latest Refit	2000
Rating	Small Expedition
Category	2-Star
Recommended For	Mature Couples
Price Point	Premium
Currency on Board	USD
Tonnage	3,963
Total Cabins	45
Inside	0
Outside	45
Balcony	0
Total Berths	96
Family Friendly?	Unsuitable
Kids Club	no
Passenger Decks	3
Wheelchair Cabins	no
Elevators	no
Dining Options	Open Dining
Casino	no
Show Lounge	no
Fitness Centre	no
Swimming Pool (internal)	no
Swimming Pool (external)	no
Self Service Laundrette	no
Cinema	no
Library	yes
Cabin Current	110 volts
Wi-Fi	no

LINDBLAD EXPEDITIONS

Ship Offering No Fly Itineraries	Lord of the Glens
Built	1988
Latest Refit	2000
Rating	3-Star
Category	Small Expedition
Recommended For	Mature Couples
Price Point	Luxury
Currency on Board	USD
Tonnage	1,065
Total Cabins	27
Inside	0
Outside	27
Balcony	0
Total Berths	54
Family Friendly?	Unsuitable
Kids Club	no
Passenger Decks	3
Wheelchair Cabins	0
Elevators	0
Dining Options	One Sitting
Casino	no
Show Lounge	0
Fitness Centre	no
Swimming Pool (internal)	0
Swimming Pool (external)	0
Self Service Laundrette	no
Cinema	no
Library	yes
Cabin Current	220 volts
Wi-Fi	no

PRINCESS CRUISES

Princess Cruises, with their 17 ships, is now considered a giant in the cruise industry. Their ships are deployed all over the world and many are repositioned to perform European itineraries during the summer.

Three ships are deployed seasonally in the 'no fly' category, the **Grand Princess**, the **Ocean Princess** & the **Crown Princess**. They are deployed out of Southampton and Dover periodically, performing a vast array of cruises from 3 to 18 days. The options are there to satisfy all of the potential 'no fly' cruisers' needs.

Princess Cruises is a mass market product very well suited to all sectors of the population and two of their large resort ships *(the Grand Princess & the Crown Princess)* are ideal for families due to the range of children's facilities on offer. The smaller Ocean Princess is more suitable for mature adults and couples as it does not have the range of children's facilities enjoyed by its sister ships.

Being an American product, English is the main language and hence favoured by Brits. Entertainment is grand, dining options varied and value for money is outstanding given the inclusions and facilities.

Princess Cruises is part of the Carnival family and the Cruise Line has enjoyed considerable success particularly in North America where a bulk of their ships are deployed. British and European passengers can seasonally enjoy the large resort ships whilst they operate on their doorstep cruising from the UK to many Mediterranean and Northern European ports.

Princess Cruises have introduced 'Personal Choice Cruising'. With personal choice you determine your own holiday schedule and tailor to your personal preferences, whims and desires. Their Personal Choice Dining program puts you in charge of your dining experience, letting you choose between restaurant–style dining *(you choose when and with whom to dine)* and the more traditional cruise ship dining arrangement with assigned table companions and staff. Depending on the ship you'll also find an alternative restaurant to please any palate.

PRINCESS CRUISES

Ship Offering No Fly Itineraries	Crown Princess	Grand Princess	Ocean Princess
Built	2006	1998	1999
Latest Refit	nil	nil	nil
Rating	4-Star	4-Star	4-Star
Category	Large Resort	Large Resort	Mid -Size
Recommended For	Families	Families	Mature Couples
Price Point	Moderate	Moderate	Moderate
Currency on Board	USD	USD	USD
Tonnage	113,000	109,000	30,277
Total Cabins	1,544	1,300	345
Inside	431	372	28
Outside	234	218	75
Balcony	879	710	242
Total Berths	3,800	3,100	824
Family Friendly?	yes	yes	no
Kids Club	yes	yes	no
Passenger Decks	15	13	9
Wheelchair Cabins	20	28	3
Elevators	14	14	4
Dining Options	Three Sittings	Three Sittings	Three Sittings
Casino	yes	yes	yes
Show Lounge	yes	yes	yes
Fitness Centre	yes	yes	yes
Swimming Pool (internal)	1	1	0
Swimming Pool (external)	3	3	1
Self Service Laundrette	yes	yes	yes
Cinema	no	no	no
Library	yes	yes	yes
Cabin Current	110 volts	110 & 220 volts	110 & 220 volts
Wi-Fi	yes	yes	yes

ROYAL CARIBBEAN INTERNATIONAL

Royal Caribbean International operates in excess of 20 ships, many of them deployed in the Americas with the focus being the Caribbean & Mexico. However, their largest ship, the *Independence of the Seas*, operates on a 'no fly' basis out of Southampton year round and is joined by the slightly smaller *Jewel of the Seas* out of Harwich during the summer.

Both ships are large resort ships well suited to all segments of the market and are particularly suitable for families as they offer great children's facilities. The Independence of the Seas at 160,000 tonnes is as long as three football fields and offers acres of deck areas, a rock climbing wall, a wave surf machine, an ice rink and a full deck totally devoted to entertaining kids.

The Jewel of the Seas, despite being a third smaller than the Independence, offers similar facilities and is perhaps more suitable to couples who are looking for a slightly more intimate experience offered by the smaller ship.

Royal Caribbean International cruise ships are some of the most innovative in the industry. They are bigger and brighter, with a lot more open spaces. Cabins with private balconies are the most available grade of cabin on offer. Nightly cabaret shows are performed in some of the largest theatres afloat. Two dinner sittings are offered daily to accommodate the entire contingent of almost 5,000 guests. If you choose not to dine in the main dining room a buffet is offered nightly on the upper deck which tends to offer a much wider choice and the dress code is far more relaxed. This is also a great option when travelling with young children.

'No fly' cruises out of the UK operated by Royal Caribbean International attract a considerable ratio of first time cruisers looking for a great value holiday, packed with fun, entertainment and great service.

ROYAL CARIBBEAN INTERNATIONAL

Ship Offering No Fly Itineraries	Independence of The Seas	Jewel of the Seas
Built	2008	2004
Latest Refit	nil	nil
Rating	4-Star	4-Star
Category	Large Resort	Large Resort
Recommended For	Families	Families
Price Point	Moderate	Moderate
Currency on Board	USD	USD
Tonnage	160,000	90,000
Total Cabins	1,817	1,050
Inside	733	237
Outside	242	236
Balcony	842	577
Total Berths	4,900	3,360
Family Friendly?	yes	yes
Kids Club	yes	yes
Passenger Decks	15	12
Wheelchair Cabins	32	14
Elevators	14	16
Dining Options	Two Sittings	Two Sittings
Casino	yes	yes
Show Lounge	yes	yes
Fitness Centre	yes	yes
Swimming Pool (internal)	0	1
Swimming Pool (external)	3	2
Self Service Laundrette	no	no
Cinema	no	yes
Library	yes	yes
Cabin Current	110 volts	110 volts
Wi-Fi	yes	yes

SAGA CRUISES

Saga specialises in providing holidays to the over 50's market and have been doing it successfully for decades. Both their ships, the *Saga Ruby* and *Saga Pearl II*, are mid size older style vessels that offer a traditional cruise experience.

Their ships are intimate and elegant and feature tastefully decorated cabins, excellent facilities and spacious decks complemented by a friendly and welcoming ambiance. Cuisine onboard is varied and plentiful and their fares are inclusive of all entertainment whilst onboard, crew gratuities, port taxes and in many instances complimentary transfers to and from Southampton & Dover.

Saga Cruises is increasingly focusing on offering more and more 'no fly' cruise itineraries departing from Southampton & Dover. The range of itineraries on offer varies in duration from 7 to 31 nights. Destinations visited vary from the Black Sea to North Africa and the Mediterranean to the Baltic States.

SAGA CRUISES

Ship Offering No Fly Itineraries	Saga Pearl II	Saga Ruby
Built	1981	1973
Latest Refit	2009	2004
Rating	Small	Mid-Size
Category	4-Star	4-Star
Recommended For	Mature Couples 50+	Mature Couples 50+
Price Point	Moderate	Moderate
Currency on Board	GBP	GBP
Tonnage	18,591	24,492
Total Cabins	258	376
Inside	82	52
Outside	178	299
Balcony	0	25
Total Berths	446	655
Family Friendly?	Unsuitable	Unsuitable
Kids Club	no	no
Passenger Decks	8	9
Wheelchair Cabins	no	4
Elevators	3	6
Dining Options	One Sitting	One Sitting
Casino	no	no
Show Lounge	yes	yes
Fitness Centre	yes	yes
Swimming Pool (internal)	1	1
Swimming Pool (external)	1	1
Self Service Laundrette	no	yes
Cinema	no	yes
Library	yes	yes
Cabin Current	220 volts	110 volts
Wi-Fi	yes	yes

SILVERSEA CRUISES

Silversea Cruises is another Cruise Line in the ultra-luxury category which appeals to passengers that demand extremely high standards. The all suite *Silver Cloud* offers three 'no fly' cruises around the British Isles and due to its size the ship can be boarded at London's Tower Bridge.

Silversea also operates the *Prince Albert II* which sails from Portsmouth to the Scottish Islands during the summer, visiting some of the best gardens and medieval castles on route. The Prince Albert II is classified as an expedition ship and despite being extremely comfortable does not offer the same luxury accommodation available aboard their other vessels.

Silversea Cruises offer deluxe cruising at the very top end of the market and has established a good reputation for a lavish fully inclusive cruising experience. Silversea ships offer excellent service, the best cuisine, superb décor and first class facilities.

SILVERSEA CRUISES

Ship Offering No Fly Itineraries	Prince Albert II	Silver Cloud
Built	1989	1994
Latest Refit	2008	nil
Rating	4-Star Plus	5-Star
Category	Small Boutique	Small Boutique
Recommended For	Mature Couples	Mature Couples
Price Point	Luxury	Ultra Luxury
Currency on Board	USD	USD
Tonnage	6,072	16,800
Total Cabins	66	150
Inside	0	0
Outside	60	38
Balcony	6	112
Total Berths	158	323
Family Friendly?	Unsuitable	Unsuitable
Kids Club	no	no
Passenger Decks	5	6
Wheelchair Cabins	0	2
Elevators	2	4
Dining Options	Open Dining	Open Dining
Casino	no	yes
Show Lounge	no	yes
Fitness Centre	yes	yes
Swimming Pool (internal)	0	0
Swimming Pool (external)	0	1
Self Service Laundrette	no	yes
Cinema	no	yes
Library	no	yes
Cabin Current	110 & 220 volts	110 & 220 volts
Wi-Fi	yes	yes

SWAN HELLENIC

Swan Hellenic operates their mid size traditional ship the *Minerva* out of Portsmouth during the summer. The 14 night cruises to the Baltic appeal to passengers wanting a smaller intimate ship, relaxed casual onboard ambiance and not as much formality as some of the other ships in this category. Each cruise itinerary is a unique, cultural travel experience, blending world-class sites with smaller off the beaten track destinations.

Swan Hellenic has a long established and renowned guest speaker programme and other daytime options include painting, writing or singing workshops, joining a yoga or tai chi class or browsing the extensive reference and fiction library and losing yourself in a good book. Evenings include fine dining, classical concerts and after dinner talks, plus occasional entertainment from ashore.

The Minerva is similar to floating country house hotel and includes all tips on board as well as tailor-made cruise books and supporting documentation.

VOYAGES OF DISCOVERY

The *MV Discovery* will be deployed from Portsmouth and Harwich in spring and summer of 2011. The voyages are from 7 to 17 nights and offer a varied choice of itineraries to France, Scandinavia & Russia and the Fjords region.

The MV Discovery appeals mainly to mature adults who are seeking a traditional cruise experience on a traditional ocean liner. Voyages of Discovery are in the moderate price category and generally appeals to an economy oriented passenger.

The MV Discovery provides cruises with more unusual and interesting itineraries and interesting port visits with knowledgeable guides and experts to provide lectures.

Voyages of Discovery is now part of All Leisure Group plc which also operates Swan Hellenic and Hebridean International Cruises.

SWAN HELLENIC CRUISES

Ship Offering No Fly Itineraries	Minerva
Built	1996
Latest Refit	2008
Rating	4-Star
Category	Small
Recommended For	Mature Couples
Price Point	Moderate
Currency on Board	GBP
Tonnage	12,500
Total Cabins	194
Inside	56
Outside	126
Balcony	12
Total Berths	474
Family Friendly?	Unsuitable
Kids Club	no
Passenger Decks	6
Wheelchair Cabins	4
Elevators	2
Dining Options	Open Dining
Casino	no
Show Lounge	yes
Fitness Centre	yes
Swimming Pool (internal)	0
Swimming Pool (external)	1
Self Service Laundrette	yes
Cinema	yes
Library	yes
Cabin Current	220 volts
Wi-Fi	no

VOYAGES OF DISCOVERY

Ship Offering No Fly Itineraries	Discovery
Built	1972
Latest Refit	2002
Rating	Small
Category	3-Star
Recommended For	Mature Couples
Price Point	Economy
Currency on Board	GBP
Tonnage	20,186
Total Cabins	351
Inside	71
Outside	280
Balcony	0
Total Berths	780
Family Friendly?	Unsuitable
Kids Club	no
Passenger Decks	8
Wheelchair Cabins	2
Elevators	4
Dining Options	Two Sittings
Casino	yes
Show Lounge	yes
Fitness Centre	yes
Swimming Pool (internal)	0
Swimming Pool (external)	2
Self Service Laundrette	no
Cinema	yes
Library	yes
Cabin Current	110 & 220 volts
Wi-Fi	no

UK 'no fly' cruising departure ports

SOUTHAMPTON

Southampton is the biggest trading and container port on the south coast of England. It has passenger ferries to the Isle of Wight and into Europe and an ever expanding cruise ship terminal. The port is also widely recognised as the capital of the cruise industry and each year more and more Cruise Lines take advantage of Southampton's superb cruise terminals. Both Southampton Railway Station and the coach station are only 1.5 miles away and Southampton is serviced by the M3 and M27 with the port clearly sign-posted.

Long term parking is available at the port and transportation from the various car parks to the ship is inclusive. Parking information can be found on www.abparking.co.uk.

We recommend that if parking is required that it is pre-booked and pre-paid as the costs are substantially lower if done in advance.

The 'no fly' Cruise Lines using Southampton are:

O *Cunard Line*
O *Celebrity Cruises*
O *Fred Olsen Cruise Lines*
O *MSC Cruises*
O *P&O Cruises*
O *Princess Cruises*
O *Regent Seven Seas*
O *Royal Caribbean International*
O *Silversea Cruises*
O *Saga Cruises*

DOVER

The town made famous by its beautiful white cliffs is located at England's closest point to continental Europe. This position, combined with an excellent harbour, has helped to make it Britain's busiest ferry port and of late many Cruise Lines have adopted Dover as their departure port.

Dover can be reached by train and the railway station is only about 5 minute taxi ride away. If driving to the port the postcode to enter into your navigation is CT17 9DQ. Ample parking is available at the port but booking in advance is recommended. Information on how to pre-book parking and any further information can be found online at www.doverport.co.uk, alternatively just ask your 'no fly' Cruise specialist at the time of booking.

The 'no fly' Cruise Lines using Dover are:

O *Classic International Cruises*
O *Costa Cruises*
O *Crystal Cruises*
O *Fred Olsen Cruise Lines*
O *Holland America Line*
O *Oceania Cruises*
O *Princess Cruises*
O *Saga Cruises*

PORTSMOUTH

Portsmouth, on the south coast of England, is a vibrant city with a proud maritime heritage. At the historic Dockyard visitors can see Admiral Nelson's HMS Victory and Henry VIII's Mary Rose. The soaring Spinnaker Tower offers stunning views over the modern naval dockyard with its frigates and destroyers, and over sweeping countryside for more than 20 miles.

Excellent road connections are available from all parts of the United Kingdom and if using a navigation system the postcode to use is PO2 8SP. You can reach Portsmouth by train from London Waterloo station, London Victoria (via Brighton) and Cardiff (via Salisbury and Bristol) to Portsmouth Harbour and Portsmouth & Southsea train stations. These stations are a short taxi ride from the port. During the summer months a bus operates between the stations and the port.

The 'no fly' Cruise Lines using Portsmouth are:

O *Compagnie du Ponant*
O *Fred Olsen Cruise Lines*
O *Hebridean Island Cruises*
O *Noble Caledonia*
O *Polar Star Expeditions*
O *Silversea Cruises*
O *Swan Hellenic*
O *Voyages of Discovery*

NEWCASTLE UPON TYNE

Newcastle is a lively and cosmopolitan city with a heritage stretching back 2,000 years. The Quayside is the symbolic and historic heart of the city. The most famous views are of the six bridges across the Tyne – the most famous yet the youngest being the Tyne Bridge (the coat-hanger) a prototype for the much larger Sydney Harbour Bridge.

Newcastle can be reached by an excellent road system from all parts of the United Kingdom and its postcode is NE29 9PT. Trains to Newcastle are available from all major cities and towns.

Long term parking at the port is available and for the best prices this should be pre-booked.

The 'no fly' Cruise Lines using Newcastle upon Tyne are:

O *Classic International Cruises*
O *Cruise & Maritime Voyages*
O *Fred Olsen Cruise Lines*

No Fly Cruising.com

TILBURY

The port of Tilbury is home to the London Cruise Terminal, the City's only deep water purpose–built cruise facility. It is located at the head of the River Thames estuary, 30 miles to the east of London, near the M25. London and its sights are the main attractions and the City can be reached by car or train.

London's principal airports – Heathrow, Gatwick, Stansted and London City Airport are within an hour's drive of the Terminal. Tilbury Town Station is on the main London Fenchurch Street to Shoeburyness line and is only a one mile away.

Long term passenger parking must be booked in advance. Information can be found on www.londoncruiseterminal.com, postcode RM18 7NG

The 'no fly' Cruise Lines using Tilbury are:

O *Cruise & Maritime Voyages*
O *Holland America Line*
O *Hebridean Island Cruises*

HARWICH

Harwich on the east coast is perfectly placed for Scandinavian and Baltic Cruises, as well as round – Britain and other European destinations. The strength of this location is its easy access to London's four airports, in particular Stansted just 50 miles away. This is complemented by excellent road links.

Rail services take passengers literally to the door of the cruise terminal. More information can be found at www.harwich.co.uk and the postcode for car satnav systems is CO12 4SR. Ample parking is available at the cruise car park.

The 'no fly' Cruise Lines using Harwich are:

O *Costa Cruises*
O *Royal Caribbean International*
O *Voyages of Discovery*

HULL

The port of Hull is in a prime location on the north bank of the River Humber. The port is one of the UK's leading foreign-trading ports. Regular cruises operate to Europe, Scandinavia and the Baltic states. The Port of Hull is the only passenger port on the Humber, handling nearly one million passengers per year and its postcode is HU9 5PQ. Long term parking is available and for further information go to: www.travel-friend.co.uk/bookingoffice_parking.htm

The 'no fly' Cruise Lines using Hull are:

O *Cruise & Maritime Voyages*

OBAN

Oban, located on the Firth of Lorn between Helensburgh and Fort William in the Argyll and Bute region of Scotland, is simply a stunning location with picturesque views all around. Oban is surrounded by beautiful beaches and breathtaking views of mountains, lochs and islands.

Travelling to Oban, on the west coast of Scotland takes approximately three hours by car, coach or train from Glasgow or Edinburgh and the postcode for your Satnav is PA34 4LW.

If you plan to travel to Oban by rail, the journey takes you along the world-famous West Highland Line. First Scot Rail runs trains three times a day from Glasgow's Queen Street Station to Oban *(two on Sunday)*

The 'no fly' Cruise Lines using Oban are:

O *Hebridean Island Cruises*

LIVERPOOL

Liverpool port has a very long maritime tradition and is convenient for customers living in the North West. A new terminal opened in 2007 and the Liverpool City Cruise Liner terminal is located on the waterfront at Princes Dock, offering first class facilities for cruise passengers. The postcode is L3 1DL.

If you are arriving by rail, Lime Street station is 4 miles away from the main cruise terminal and frequent services to London and other major UK cities is available.

The 'no fly' Cruise Lines using Liverpool are:

O *Cruise & Maritime Voyages*
O *Fred Olsen Cruise Lines*

No Fly Cruising.com

ROSYTH

The port of Rosyth is located on the Forth Estuary some 8 miles from Edinburgh.

Easy access is available by road from most regions of the UK and the port's postcode is KY11 2XP. If you are arriving by train then Inverkeithing is the nearest train station to the Rosyth Cruise Port. Frequent train services are available to and from Edinburgh and there is a shuttle bus service which links Rosyth Cruise Port with Inverkeithing train station. Rosyth Cruise port provides ample short and long term car parking facilities.

The 'no fly' Cruise Lines using Rosyth are:

O *Classic International Cruises*
O *Fred Olsen Cruise Lines*

GREENOCK

Greenock used to be an industrial port and shipyard but is nowadays a growing UK cruise port. Greenock Ocean terminal is located less than one mile from the city centre. The port of Greenock can easily be reached by road from all parts of the UK and the postcode is PA16 8UU.

For rail travellers Greenock Station and Greenock West Station can be reached via a short taxi ride from the port. Both Greenock stations are well connected to Glasgow Central Station. Ample long and short term parking is available at the port of Greenock.

The 'no fly' Cruise Lines using Greenock are:

O *Cunard Line*
O *Fred Olsen Cruise Lines*
O *Hebridean Island Cruises*
O *Silversea Cruises*

EDINBURGH

Leith has for centuries acted as the port of Edinburgh and remains one of Scotland's larger ports. The modern harbour is located in South Leith. Redevelopment from the early 1990s has resulted in the largest water-front development in Europe, including the Scottish Executive building at Victoria Quay, desirable residential dwellings, retail and leisure facilities including the Ocean Terminal Complex which incorporates the permanent berth of the Royal Yacht Britannia.

The port can be reached by taxi from the Edinburgh city centre and its postcode is EH6 7DN.

The 'no fly' Cruise Lines using Edinburgh are:

O *Cruise & Maritime Voyages*
O *Hebridean Island Cruises*
O *Noble Caledonia*
O *Silversea Cruises*

DUBLIN

The port of Dublin is the largest port in Ireland and is very centrally located, being only minutes from Dublin city centre. Buses and taxis provide a regular service from the city to Dublin Cruise terminal, which is located at Alexandra Quay.

The 'no fly' Cruise Lines using Dublin are:

O *Cruise & Maritime Voyages*

FALMOUTH

Falmouth is a resort and port located on the southern Cornish coast at the entrance to the large and sheltered natural harbour of Carrick Roads.

The port can be reached from most parts of the UK by road and its postcode is TR11 3JQ.

The 'no fly' Cruise Lines using Falmouth are:

O *Cruise & Maritime Voyages*

CARDIFF

Cardiff is the capital city of Wales and lies at the mouth of the Taff and Ely rivers. The Port of Cardiff is located adjacent to Cardiff Bay at postcode CF10 4LY and is just under 1 mile from the city centre. If you are arriving by train the Cardiff Central rail station is approximately 1 mile away and taxis are readily available.

The 'no fly' Cruise Lines using Cardiff are:

O *Hebridean Island Cruises*

FAIRLIE

Fairlie lies on the Atlantic Coast of Scotland to the southwest of Glasgow. It sits on the eastern shore of the Firth of Clyde and looks across to the Isle of Arran and the Cumbraes. Fairlie can be reached by road from all parts of Scotland and is at postcode KA29 0AS.

The 'no fly' Cruise Lines using Fairlie are:

O *Hebridean Island Cruises*

INVERGORDON

Invergordon is a deepwater port near the entrance of Cromarty Firths "the seaway to the Scottish Highlands". Inverness is the capital of the Highlands and is half an hour from Invergordon by road and Loch Ness is just a few miles beyond.

There isn't much to the cruise terminal, as it consists mainly of a pier with room for ships as large as the QE2. The port can be reached by road from most parts of Scotland and is at postcode IV18 0HD.

The 'no fly' Cruise Lines using Invergordon are:

O *Hebridean Island Cruises*

INVERNESS

Set on the Moray where the Caledonian Canal meets the sea via the River Ness, this historic town is close to Loch Ness and Culloden Battlefield.

Inverness can be conveniently reached by road from all parts of Scotland.

The 'no fly' Cruise Lines using Inverness are:

O *Lindblad Expeditions*

How to get the best deal on your 'no fly' cruise holiday

How to read the Cruise Lines' brochure

The Cruise Lines are multi-million pound businesses and spend a considerable amount of money promoting their ships to the general public. This is shown in the glossy television commercials and brochures, which are designed to entice prospective customers with the glamour of cruising.

Their marketing is focused to entice the customers they would like to appeal to, not necessarily those that predominantly cruise. Therefore, most advertising and brochure shots feature attractive middle-aged adults and a broad spectrum of family groups enjoying the very best facilities on board.

No Cruise Line goes out to deliberately mislead *(that would be a very poor short term strategy)*, but in all instances they are likely to put a very positive spin on things. So, as long as you are aware of that and take their marketing with a pinch of salt, their brochures are extremely informative.

They will show you details of the cabins *(but won't mention which ones suffer the most noise from their proximity to late night bars and discos)*, restaurants and facilities. They will have deck plans and itineraries and here it is useful to look at cruises that you are considering ensuring that they go to the ports you wish to visit and that they stop for sufficient time for you to disembark and enjoy the destination in more than just a cursory way.

And, of course, they include the cruise price. But as I am sure you are more than aware brochure price should only be used to compare one cruise against another as cruise prices are constantly flexing dependent on factors such as demand, currency and fuel fluctuations and of course very different deals available through different agencies.

Who's Who in the selling game

The cruise industry has grown massively over the last couple of decades and has doubled in size over the last ten years. With the Cruise Lines' investment in new ships and new capacity coming on stream on a pretty much constant basis the industry has to continue growing at a double digit rate in order to pay back their investment. With the new ships has come a new market of younger families and couples looking at cruise ships as a resort holiday, rather than a cruise in the traditional sense of the word.

Currently 80% of all cruises are sold by companies other than the Cruise Lines. This percentage has little changed over recent times and as a result when the Cruise Line set their prices *(and discounts)* they offer this to all of the companies and chains in the distribution channel. So, theoretically you should be able to buy the same cruise at exactly the same rate from a travel agent, website or cruise specialist. However there are pros and cons to each seller.

> *There has never been a better time to book a 'no fly' cruise; the choice is wider than ever and the price has never been more affordable*

The Cruise Lines

The Cruise Lines all have their own sales departments and are happy to take bookings online or over the phone with customers direct. If you are a seasoned cruiser and know precisely what you want then this is not necessarily a bad place to book.

However, the Cruise Line is only there to sell their ships and they have no interest in recommending their competitors if the ship is likely to be unsuitable for your particular needs.

In addition, the Cruise Lines have an agreement with the travel trade that they will not undercut the prices that customers are able to get for the same cruise through agencies, so there is no financial incentive to book direct with the Cruise Line.

Wholesalers

In the cruising market large volume wholesalers purchase cabins from Cruise Lines in bulk and then mark these up to sell either direct to the public or through travel agents. Many of these wholesalers are internet based and only offer specific cruises at cheap rates, rather than all available cruises, as they generally only deal with the large Cruise Lines.

But remember, they will steer you towards the cruises that they have the best margin on, or the most cabins to shift, and not necessarily to those that are the best option for you.

Travel Agents

The cruise industry growth has been built on the expertise, knowledge and enthusiasm of the travel agency network. They have effectively been, over the last few decades, the Cruise Lines' shop window.

However, with increased rent and rates and the impact of internet sellers many of the best independent travel agents have gone out of business, leaving the high street travel agents pretty much exclusively owned by Thomas Cook, Thomson and a number of independent chains such as Co-operative Travel.

This has brought into sharp contrast the problem with this distribution channel; in that the staff are required to have the knowledge to try and sell everything from a luxury cruise, to a package holiday in Spain, a skiing holiday or a weekend City break and everything in-between. Inevitably staff will make the easiest sale and take direction from head office as to what they should be promoting, rather than considering all options available and allowing the customer to reach the right decision for them.

Some high street travel agents do employ cruise specialists, but again their knowledge is spread across all cruise options, with fly cruising often offering them enhanced commissions. There are very few 'no fly' cruise specialists.

Travel agencies earn a commission from the Cruise Lines for every booking that they make, with many of the large agencies able to achieve what are called over-ride commissions if they hit certain levels of volume sales. This again inevitably leads to the agent recommending one Cruise Line over another, not because it is the best option for you, but because it generates the most commission for them or contributes to them achieving their volume targets.

Internet Agencies

These have grown rapidly over the last few years and a majority of press advertising is placed by specialist web companies who may or may not specialise in cruises, and certainly do not specialise in 'no fly' cruising. However, only 16% of all cruises are booked online and the reason why this figure will continue to only grow slowly is that a cruise is not a 'commodity' like a flight or a widget; it is a holiday that can be infinitely personalised to suit you.

What they do specialise in is maximising their volume of sales and using their low cost base to offer prices in the market that may not be available when you come to book (*this is normally because only a limited number of cabins at that grade and at that price are available in the first place*).

It is always wise to phone up the company and talk to one of their sales people. Satisfy yourself that you are being given the best possible advice and that the price advertised is the one that you end up paying. If there is not the opportunity to speak to someone direct and the only way to get the advertised low price is to buy online then our advice is to walk away. It is invariably the case that these great prices are available on late deals and so if there is a problem you will have no easy way of resolving it if you have not established a relationship with a professional cruise specialist.

> *If booking on the internet, make sure that you can speak to a specialist on the telephone should the need arise as mistakes are sometimes difficult to rectify.*

Online auctions

This is a relatively new phenomenon and is starting to creep over from America. This is where a cruise is offered for sale and holidaymakers 'bid' to get it at a discounted price.

The main issue here is that as with all auctions you have to decide a price that you are prepared to pay and then stick to it! But that's the difficult part, as auction sites work on the basis that bidders get caught up in the process and can end up paying more than the cruise is actually worth.

'No Fly' Cruise Specialists

Unsurprisingly, this is the route that we would recommend that you go down when booking your 'no fly' cruise holiday. 'No fly' Cruise consultants are specialists in this sector and can invariably advise you best with regard to which Cruise Line and ship would best suit your needs. They are more consistently in contact with the 'no fly' market and cruise lines themselves and so their knowledge tends to be more up to date and relevant. They should also be able to offer you the best price, or at least match the best price in the market. Above all, a cruise specialist is looking to retain you as a customer for life. If they can ensure that your first cruise is right, they know that the chances are that you will be hooked on cruising and will look for the same advice and good service from your 'no fly' cruise specialist as you had experienced before.

> *No fly' cruise specialists unsurprisingly specialise in the 'no fly' cruise market and so are likely to offer the most expert and up to date advice.*

NoFlyCruising.com

The Discount Maze

One of the major problems in choosing a cruise at the moment is that there is a bewildering array of discounts and incentives, all seeming to offer outstanding value for money… for a limited time only!

Full page ads in all the major national newspapers offering specific cruises at introductory prices, early booking discounts, free flights, free upgrades, on-board spend, group discounts, late availability with unbelievable prices and more.

It can be confusing and even when you've paid for your cruise you can sometimes feel as though you can never be sure that you've got the best deal.

Essentially this confusion and seemingly constant discounting has arisen because of the massive increase in cabins available with the new ships coming on line in the last ten years. A cabin is the ultimate perishable commodity in that once the ship sails what was worth £1,000 one day, becomes worthless the next. So Cruise Lines look at an individual cruise and decide what they would like the average price that each customer needs to pay to be, and they will then use a number of marketing and pricing mechanisms to achieve that average.

They want to get a sizable percentage of customers to commit early and they will offer early booking discounts and loyalty incentives in order to achieve that. During the middle phase of the booking process the price will revert more towards a brochure price, with late availability discounts coming into play as the cruise departure date looms closer – with the level of those discounts varying depending on their success in filling that particular cruise up to that point *(but beware, if they have been successful in marketing the cruise there may not be any availability at all)*.

At the end of the day, you have to choose a cruise that you want to go on - with the Cruise Line that appeals to you - on the ship that offers you the best overall array of facilities and style of cruise that suits your requirements. You can then look at the available itineraries and cruise durations to further filter your search. Then, and only then, are you able to look for the best price.

> *Remember, a bargain is not a bargain if you end up compromising on the holiday you want in order to secure a slightly better price.*

But, given all that you should still look to get the best possible price for the cruise that you want and so the following is an explanation of the major discounts and incentives that are used in the market.

Early booking discounts
The size and variety of these discounts is variable by Cruise Line and can be turned off very quickly. Essentially if you book more than nine months in advance of your cruise departure date, you should be looking for an early booking discount.

Alternatively Cruise Lines will offer an early booking discount off cruises booked before a specific date. In the UK this tends to be around the end of January as more cruise holidays are sold in January than in any other month of the year.

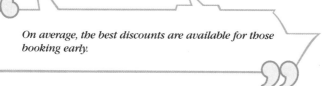

> On average, the best discounts are available for those booking early.

Discounts off additional passengers
'Two for one' offers are generally only offered when a cruise needs to boost its bookings and will only be offered for a short period of time. But do be careful, 'two for one' is not always the same as half price – for example a cruise could define a single person rate as being the 'one' (this would include a single person supplement) which is obviously more expensive than the double occupancy rate divided by two.

50% off the second passenger in a cabin is a great headline discount but is actually only 25% off per person.

Discounts or free places for more than two sharing a cabin are fairly standard and are normally offered year round. These are particularly popular with families who are happy for two adults and two children to share a cabin. However, this can become somewhat claustrophobic with adults or teenagers and may end up being a false economy, so if this is appealing to you then do discuss this in detail with your 'no fly' cruise specialist and they will be able to advise you of the best cabin grades for your requirements.

Free days
This is where discount is hidden by offering a cruise of say 9 nights for the price of 7. Alternatively the Cruise Line may offer two back to back cruises with slightly different itineraries at a discount in order to encourage single week cruisers to take a longer 14 night option.

Free upgrades

These can be offered to early bookers as a way of encouraging you to upgrade from the basic cabin category for a discounted price. This has the added benefit to the Cruise Line of freeing up these base cabin types for late availability discounts.

Upgrades are only offered by Cruise Lines on sailings that are liable to depart without reaching full capacity. Full sailings almost never offer cabin upgrades and so don't be disappointed if you are unable to upgrade close to the departure date. If a Cruise Line does offer upgrades they are likely to do so to the earliest bookers first.

When a ship has sold out of a certain cabin category, they may offer a guarantee. This is where the customer pays for the grade that they wish and the ship guarantees that they will get this grade, or better. If your cruise specialist insinuates that this is a certain method of achieving a free upgrade, do not believe them. All that is happening is that the Cruise Line is double selling a cabin on the basis that they know a certain percentage of customers will cancel before the sailing. They are pretty good at this calculation and so you are unlikely to get 'bumped' up a category.

One final 'free upgrade' discount mechanism that is sometimes used is what is referred to as 'flat rates'. This is where the Cruise Line will offer all cabins (except probably the most luxurious) at a single flat rate with the best cabins going to the earliest bookers.

> *The best chance of achieving a low cost upgrade is to book early and take advantage of the offers available at that time.*

Discounted or free transportation to port

This is where the Cruise Line offers discounted coach, rail fare or parking.

Repositioning cruises

Ships 'migrate' around the world, offering cruises to local markets to ensure that they are as full as they possibly can be at all times. A repositioning cruise is when a ship sails from one part of the world to another. There are often large discounts available, as these cruises tend to spend a disproportionate time at sea crossing the major oceans, which does not appeal to the majority of cruisers. But if this appeals to you then seek these out.

Group discounts

If you are travelling in a group of ten or more then you may be able to negotiate a special 'group rate' that could include one free place for the group organiser, plus discounts and potential upgrades. The earlier you book your group the better as this represents guaranteed business for the Cruise Line before they have sold out through the general market.

Some agents will offer special group rates for volume as this helps them in their negotiations with the Cruise Lines. So, if you can gather friends together it may be extremely worthwhile to consider being a group organiser.

Late availability discounts

These are often the best prices you can get, BUT you may not get your preferred cruise, ship or even Cruise Line. If price over-rides your concern for the type and style of cruise you want then this may be the best strategy. However, in almost all instances the advice is to book early to get the best cruise options at the best price.

Price matching

Many travel agents and internet sellers will guarantee to price match if you are able to beat their quote. However, the terms and conditions attached to such offers tend to be restrictive. Even if you do manage to get the price match it will inevitably only represent a small percentage of the available purchase price. Remember, your cruise specialist or travel agent needs to make money or they will not be your specialist for long!

> *When looking to secure the best possible price always compare apples with apples! A 7 night luxury cruise will never be comparable to a holiday on a more modest ship.*

No Fly Cruising.com

5 Handy Hints to follow when booking your 'no fly' cruise

1. Find a 'no fly' cruise specialist

The importance here is to find a specialist who knows the market – so if you are looking at a 'no fly' cruise then a consultant that specialises in 'no fly' cruising is the sensible first place to start.

2. Narrow down your choice

Use your 'no fly' cruise specialist's knowledge to narrow down your potential shortlist of ideal cruises.

3. Check prices

Ask your 'no fly' cruise specialist to quote you the best available price or prices for the cruise(s) you have selected. Then it is always advisable to have an understanding of what prices are available through other sources – but remember, you only have a few hours at best to do this as Cruise Line's no longer hold 'options' and so a price may only be valid for a very short period of time.

4. Push your specialist to better the best price available

If you have found a better price for the cruise that you wish to buy, then do go back to where you booked and ask whether they are able to match that price. But remember, if there is only a small difference you may be asking a specialist to forgo their commission to secure the sale – bear in mind that this may even affect the level of service that they can afford you in the long run.

5. Protect yourself

Make sure that the insurance you buy covers you for everything that you need; particularly cancellation protection. Your 'no fly' cruise specialist will be able to advise you on this but the prices charged can vary widely so do a little bit of investigation. Above all, make sure that any policy you buy is underwritten by a well known company of repute and that you are truthful when declaring pre-existing medical conditions – if you need to make a claim even a slight variation to the conditions of the policy could end up being very expensive.

Life on board

Life on board your cruise ship will depend on the Cruise Line, ship size, itinerary and style of cruise you have chosen. There are cruises designed to suit virtually every interest and personal preference.

The choices include: luxury cruises; large, contemporary ships with a fantastic array of recreational facilities; Mid-Size to smaller ships which have a more personal touch; classic vessels which are very traditional; special-interest or exploration cruises specialising in unique destinations with an accent on cultural enrichment.

For many, the perfect holiday includes the non-stop fun and sun of a resort-style cruise to the Mediterranean or Caribbean, where you can sample a variety of island cultures and cuisines while relaxing in style.

> *Many Cruise Lines create special "themes" on-board, with entertainment ranging from jazz festivals to murder mysteries at sea! If you are looking for something in particular then discuss this with your 'no fly' cruise specialist.*

Are all ships fairly similar?
Size does matter. Cruise ships range from intimate and yacht-like vessels catering for up to 100 passengers to ships stretching longer than three football fields where up to 4,900 passengers are on board. The facilities on board will also vary from ship to ship; you can enjoy atmospheres ranging from casual to formal, contemporary to classic. Enjoy the endless activities offered on a contemporary resort-style cruise from climbing walls and ice rinks to smaller ships where you have more of a personal and relaxed atmosphere.

Are there different classes of service?
Most cruise ships today are "one-class" where everyone can use all of the ship's facilities. The price is primarily based on the cabin size and location. Regardless of the category you book, you'll enjoy the same menus, activities and entertainment as everyone else on board. The Cunard Line is the only exception to this as your restaurant is assigned dependent on the cabin booked.

Cabin types
There are several different grades of cabin on board cruise ships and this is the main factor that determines the cost of the cruise. All cabins have a separate bathroom

with shower washbasin and toilet. Higher cabin grades normally have a full size bath, mini bar, fridge and personal safe. All cabin grades have supplies of soap, shampoo, conditioner and towels.

A basic guideline for cabin types:

Interior cabins
This is the standard cabin and is normally what the lowest (often published) cruise fare is based on. The cabins are situated on the inside of the ship so you have no windows or port holes for natural light. The cabin can be quite compact but has sufficient space for bed and separate bathroom with shower. These cabins are not suitable if you feel uncomfortable with no natural light.

Outside cabins
These are usually slightly bigger than inside cabins but will either have a port hole or a window. Some will have a shower in the bathroom while some will have a bathtub.

Superior outside cabins have a picture window and a bathtub in the bathroom, you can also get junior suites/deluxe suites which will be larger in size and have a separate bedroom and sitting area.

Balcony cabins
There are several types of cabins with a Balcony; superior suites, mini suites, marquee suite, deluxe suite, premier suites and many more. They differ in size, facilities, size of balconies and location.

Suites are obviously the most luxurious and spacious and most come with butler service, plus a lounge or sitting room separated from the bedroom. On more modern recently built ships balcony cabins account for 60% – 80% of all the ship's accommodation.

The benefit with balcony cabins is you can sit and enjoy the view or even have dinner arranged on the balcony. Some can be small and can't accommodate two chairs, they may also only be separated from the adjacent cabin's balcony by a full floor to ceiling screen, so are not as private as they could be.

You also have to consider the location of balcony cabins on the ship; if on the bow side they may face forward and can be subject to wind whereas stern balconies are generally more protected. Other balconies are covered providing shade and privacy while others maybe open to the weather, but perfect for sunbathing.

Some ships also have French balconies which have doors to open for fresh air and a great sea view, but you are unable to sit on them.

Location of cabins

The higher the deck the higher the cabin price normally is. You also have to consider the location of the cabin on the ship as this will make a difference.

If you are looking for a quiet location then make sure it is not above the late bars and disco.

If you have difficulty with walking distances then ask for a cabin mid-ship as this will be nearer the lifts. Mid-ship cabins are also normally more stable, less noisy and vibration free. Ships powered by diesel *(which is most modern ships)* create and transmit some vibration, especially at the stern during manoeuvring.

Cabins situated at the front of the ships can be slightly crescent-shaped and exposed to early morning noise such as the anchor being dropped at ports where the ship is too big to dock. Lower decks can be subject to heat and tend to be closer to any engine noise.

> *Your 'no fly' cruise specialist can advise you on the best cabin to suit your needs and will confirm your specific cabin number with the Cruise Line at the time of booking.*

Finding your feet *(especially on large ships)*

When you first arrive in your cabin after embarkation your luggage will probably not be delivered for a few hours, so you should take this opportunity to find your bearings on board the ship. You will have been given a detailed map of the ship when you checked in so using this you should start to find the location of different decks, restaurants, bars, entertainment, pools etc. It is also wise to find the quickest route to your cabin as the ships are vast in size and you will probably walk endless miles in the first few days finding your way around.

Will I be cruising with like-minded people?

There's no such thing as a typical cruise passenger! All kinds of people take cruises; all ages, from all walks of life, singles, couples and families. However, because a 'no fly' cruise departs from and returns to a UK port, the vast majority of your fellow cruisers will be British. The cruises are designed to appeal to the culinary and cultural tastes of British citizens so you will be sailing with fellow travellers who are likely to have shared values and interests to those of your own.

Just ask your 'no fly' cruise specialist for advice on the best ship for you based on your tastes and lifestyle.

Do Cruise Lines welcome families with kids?

More and more cruise holidays are booked by families with children. Most Cruise Lines provide plenty of supervised activities for kids especially during school holidays. If your children enjoy swimming, sports, games, movies and the adventure of new places, they'll love a family cruise. Ships even offer different types of age-appropriate activities suitable for toddlers to teens. Best of all, children often travel at a reduced rate. The youth counsellors will also help keep them busy and entertained.

> *Before deciding on what ship best suits your family ensure that you tell your 'no fly' cruise specialist of your specific wishes so that these can be matched to the right ship.*

Booking a cruise holiday without the 'little darlings'

If you are looking for cruises for adults only then these are also available with selected Cruise Lines on specific ships and dates. In addition the larger ships cater for families and adults and will have 'adult' only sections on the ship, for example pool areas and bars, so if you are looking to enjoy some 'adult' time you are able to find this onboard a larger ship.

So after deciding what ship, which destination, which cabin type etc, here is some information that will help with embarkation, disembarking and a general overview as to what to expect 'on board'.

What are the restrictions on luggage?

One of the benefits of 'No Fly Cruising' is you can take considerably more luggage than if you were to fly. But you do need to consider the storage space in the cabin as it may be more restricted than the amount of luggage you have packed!!

What should you pack?

Again this can depend on the cruise ship and the destinations. Many Cruise Lines now feature a more relaxed and casual approach to dress throughout the cruise - while on others, formal dinners or parties are part of the fun.

Cruise holidays are generally casual by day, whether you're on the ship or ashore, but in the evening the ship's dress codes may vary. As a guideline short 3-4 night cruises will have one formal, one informal and one or two casual nights. One week cruises will have one or two formal, two informal then two or three casual nights. On two week cruises there will generally be two to four formal nights, four to six informal and four or five casual nights.

As a general guideline cruise ships class formal for men as Black Tie or dark suit with tie, and for the ladies an evening gown or cocktail dress. But if you don't own a Black Tie it is not necessary to purchase this just for the trip as a dark suit and tie is perfectly acceptable on most large ships.

Informal for men would be long trousers, collared shirt and tie and for the ladies a dress or similar smart attire. Casual / relaxed for men would be long trousers but tie optional and ladies a more casual dress or outfit.

> *Formal evenings on ships can be grand but you don't need to rush out to buy Black Tie, a dark suit is perfectly acceptable on most ships.*

Embarkation

Your embarkation time will be stated on your cruise documents. Don't arrive prior to the time on the ticket as you will not be permitted to board the ship, but don't leave it too late as the gangway closes 30-60 minutes prior to sailing time.

When you arrive at the port and enter the embarkation building your luggage will be X-rayed and you will probably be asked for identification.

The desks in the passenger terminal are normally alphabetical; go to the one that displays the first letter of your surname to 'check in'. After completing all the embarkation, registration and immigration documents you will be given a colour coded embarkation card or number card, as embarkation is normally processed in batches of approximately 100 passengers at a time. When boarding the ship you will have your photograph taken and this will be loaded into the Cruise Line identification security system together with your booking details.

You will either be escorted to your cabin or pointed in the general direction.

Compulsory passenger lifeboat drill will take place within the first 24 hours after the ship sails from the embarkation port.

> *Don't try to smuggle bottles of liquor in your cases, these will be picked up and confiscated by the security personnel.*

NoFlyCruising.com

What about meal times?
During the day, there are many different places to eat - in the formal dining room, on deck, in a pizzeria or at an espresso bar to name just a few.

In the evenings some ships offer 'flexible' eating and 'open' seating which means you can sit and eat where you want within the opening hours of the dining room. On ships without 'open seating', unless you are with your family or a group, you will be seated next to strangers. The Cruise Lines are geared to accommodate each guest's wishes, and it is possible to request a table for two or four. In the unlikely event that you do wish to change tablemates, speak with the maitre d', who will make every effort to seat you with more compatible dining companions.

Depending on the size of the ship you may have one, two or four sittings as dining rooms cannot accommodate all guests at one time. More traditional ships have two sittings in their formal dining rooms, which differ only by time: typically 6:00 p.m. and 8:30 p.m. To choose, just decide whether you prefer to dine early or late and then tell your 'no fly' cruise specialist your preference when you book your cruise. Experienced cruisers say they prefer sitting at a table with several other diners; some lifelong friendships have been made this way.

> *The later dining option is generally more popular so ensure this is booked for you at the same time as your cabin.*

Alternative dining might also be available but this would incur an extra cost of approximately £5-£35 per person. Alternative dining offers a more intimate and quieter dining experience with a good ambience and choice of menu. However be aware that as well as the initial additional meal and wine cost there will also be an extra cover charge, which soon mounts up during the duration of the cruise.

More and more Cruise Lines are opening up their informal lido areas to evening dining where the dress and dishes are casual. You can even eat out under the stars and a large number of ships offer romantic in-cabin dinners. The choice is yours!

Special diets
Most ships can accommodate salt-free, low-carbohydrate, low cholesterol, Kosher, or other dietary preferences. However this request must be made in advance so be sure to advise your 'no fly' cruise specialist when you book your cruise.

No Fly Cruising.com

Drink prices

The costs of drinks on board are normally lower than on land since ships have access to duty free alcohol. Dining rooms normally have extensive and reasonably priced wine lists but some Cruise Lines will also add a cover charge of approximately 15% to the bill.

Some ships also sell duty free wine and alcohol which you may be able drink in your cabin; however this may not be taken into the dining or public areas. This protects the bar sales which is a substantial source of onboard revenue. When purchasing duty free alcohol either on the ship or in port this will be stored for you until the last day of the cruise then returned to you prior to disembarkation.

Are there no-smoking areas?

Virtually all ships have smoking and non-smoking sections in some public rooms and on deck. In fact many dining rooms and even some entire ships are now totally smoke-free, reflecting passenger preferences. Some Cruise Lines permit smoking in cabins but other companies may only allow this in cabins with balconies.

What's there to do at night?

When the stars come out, a cruise ship really comes alive. There's dancing, live entertainment, nightclubs and lounges, feature films and parties. Most ships also have casinos. What's more, there are many special events like the Captain's Cocktail Party, Passenger Talent Night and it's all free. The shows are live, films first-rate and all included in your cruise fare.

Remember it is your holiday and you can do as much or as little as you want to. Most importantly relax and have a great time!

On a cruise, you do what you want when you want. You can do everything or do absolutely nothing. It's your holiday!

Learning experiences and special educational programmes

Many Cruise Lines feature an extensive programme of on-board enrichment seminars hosted by distinguished guest experts. In addition to lectures highlighting the history and sights of ports you will be visiting.

Some cruise companies specialise in Adventure and Expeditions. These ships tend to be smaller and less formal than the bigger cruise ships and the itineraries and programmes are very specific. They are aimed at experienced travellers who prefer an educational environment and do not want all the activities and entertainment typical of mainstream cruises.

Other facilities on board
All large cruise ships have a wide range of day time activities ranging from fully equipped fitness gyms, exercise and dance classes for the more active passengers to spa's massages and body treatments, steam rooms and saunas for the passengers who want to unwind and relax. Not forgetting the onboard swimming pools and decks where you can top up your tan or catch up on your reading.

> *Extra charges do mount up so if you are concerned then remember you can ask for a balance from the cruise manager at any time.*

What about tipping?
Tipping is a matter of individual preference and most Cruise Lines now publish guidelines in their brochures. A general rule is to plan for a total of approximately £4 - £7 per person per day. Some Cruise Lines will automatically add gratuities to your onboard account which can be adjusted if required when the account is paid at the end of the cruise. Gratuities are sometimes included in the cruise fare, normally those at the luxury end of the market, where no tipping is permitted – at least that is the theory!

Extra charges onboard
Although all the entertainment and food is included in the price you do have to be aware of some additional expenses that you need to budget for as these could soon add up.

Shore excursions are bookable prior to your cruise and also when you have boarded and the price will vary depending on the excursion. Drinks on board during the cruise, although they are reasonably priced will mount up and also remember 10–15% can be added for wine ordered in the restaurant.

Additional costs could include laundry, spa treatments, alternative dining, internet access, medical costs and duty free shopping both on board and in destinations.

Are there medical services onboard?

Virtually every cruise ship *(except for some smaller vessels operating in coastal waters)* has a medical facility and health care professionals on staff which will normally consist of a doctor and two nurses who would be able to handle almost any emergency.

One of the most common concerns for passenger's especially first time cruisers is suffering from sea sickness!

Today's ships have stabilizers which should reduce the effects of sea sickness and as a result less than 3% of passengers suffer. A good tip to try if you notice the first movement of the ship is to walk back and forth on the deck. You will start to find your knees, your natural form of stabilizers which will start to get their feel of balance. This is known as getting your 'sea legs'!

Alternatively you could try pressure pads that can be purchased from a pharmacy or chewing ginger tablets. As a last resort, the ship's Doctor can prescribe a more powerful remedy; however that would be at your own expense.

Communication with the outside world

Most ships have a daily newsletter with news, headlines, selected stock quotes and sports results and many cabins are equipped with televisions and have satellite or cellular telephones. New ships all have the technology to enable passengers to use their own personal mobile telephone with the cost being charged to the mobile account. But beware this can be expensive. The best and cheapest way to keep in touch with family and friends is to use e-mail as most ships have an internet cafe. Alternatively send e-mails while in port as this would be a lot less expensive than onboard.

Onboard internet uses satellites for connection so costs can quickly mount up if used excessively.

Shopping onboard / Duty free

Shops onboard cruise ships are duty free and competitive in price. A variety of shops can be found such as jewellery, gifts, accessories, fragrance & cosmetics, fashion, necessities and alcohol. So whatever you have forgotten to pack something or if you want to treat yourself you will be able to purchase while onboard. Be aware though that the shops onboard are normally closed while in port due to international customs regulations.

Certain Cruise Lines may allow you to bring a bottle of wine or champagne to drink in your cabin, however it would not be permitted to be taken into dining areas and any public areas to drink. All alcohol purchased while onboard or from a port will be kept for you and returned prior to disembarkation.

Paying your onboard account

It is now normal for all Cruise Lines to operate cash-free cruising so all purchases and expenditure will be added to your personal account. When you board the ship an imprint of a credit card will be taken to ensure you can cover any onboard expenses. Throughout the cruise you sign for everything. Some cruise ships have the facility to check the balance of your account on the television in the cabin. All cruise ships will deliver a detailed statement to your cabin the day prior to disembarkation. Some Cruise Lines may discontinue their 'cashless' system on the last day of the cruise, some may also add a currency conversion service charge to your credit card if not in the same currency as the Cruise Line.

> *If you don't have a credit card the Cruise Line may request that you lodge a cash deposit prior to embarkation. This may need to be topped up if used up during the cruise, and any unspent amount will be refunded at the end of your cruise.*

Disembarkation

Disembarkation can be the most tiring and seemingly rushed part of the cruise.

An informal talk on customs, immigration and disembarkation procedures will have been given the previous day by the cruise director and customs forms given out to complete. Include any duty free items purchased either aboard or ashore *(keep all receipts in case a customs officer asks for them)* and complete coloured tags, which will also have been distributed.

The night before your disembarkation you must place all luggage, apart from hand luggage, outside the cabin door before 2.00am. This enables it to be collected and off loaded on arrival the next day which can take between two to three hours. No passenger is allowed to leave the ship until all the baggage has been offloaded.

Breakfast is normally served early as the ship will dock between 7.00am and 8.00am and, as with many hotels, ships have a fast check out procedure as they only have approximately four hours to prepare the ship for the next passengers boarding.

Disembarking can either be organised by colour coded tags so about 100 passengers can be disembarked at a time or the cruise ship may ask you to vacate your cabin at a certain time and wait in one of the public areas.

Your first stop will be at immigration and then onto the baggage holding area where you will identify your luggage and take it to the customs area. There you may need to produce your duty free purchases and receipts if requested.

After clearing customs you are then able to make your way to your selected transport home.

16 things that the glossy brochures won't tell you....

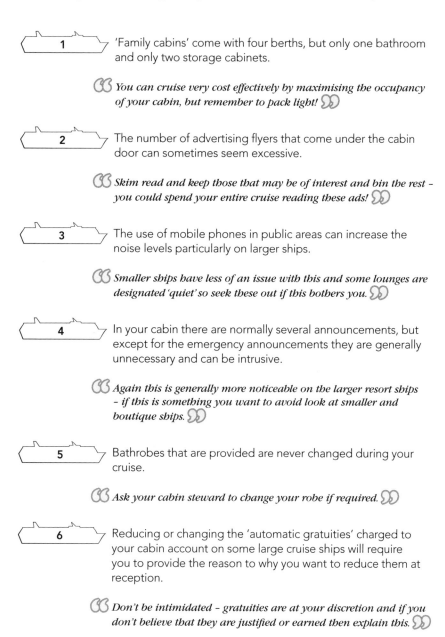

1 'Family cabins' come with four berths, but only one bathroom and only two storage cabinets.

You can cruise very cost effectively by maximising the occupancy of your cabin, but remember to pack light!

2 The number of advertising flyers that come under the cabin door can sometimes seem excessive.

Skim read and keep those that may be of interest and bin the rest – you could spend your entire cruise reading these ads!

3 The use of mobile phones in public areas can increase the noise levels particularly on larger ships.

Smaller ships have less of an issue with this and some lounges are designated 'quiet' so seek these out if this bothers you.

4 In your cabin there are normally several announcements, but except for the emergency announcements they are generally unnecessary and can be intrusive.

Again this is generally more noticeable on the larger resort ships – if this is something you want to avoid look at smaller and boutique ships.

5 Bathrobes that are provided are never changed during your cruise.

Ask your cabin steward to change your robe if required.

6 Reducing or changing the 'automatic gratuities' charged to your cabin account on some large cruise ships will require you to provide the reason to why you want to reduce them at reception.

Don't be intimidated – gratuities are at your discretion and if you don't believe that they are justified or earned then explain this.

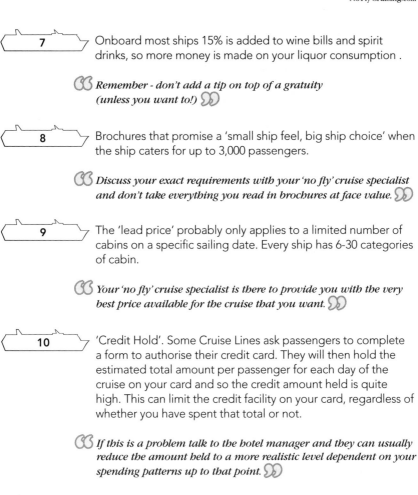

7   Onboard most ships 15% is added to wine bills and spirit drinks, so more money is made on your liquor consumption .

Remember - don't add a tip on top of a gratuity (unless you want to!)

8   Brochures that promise a 'small ship feel, big ship choice' when the ship caters for up to 3,000 passengers.

Discuss your exact requirements with your 'no fly' cruise specialist and don't take everything you read in brochures at face value.

9   The 'lead price' probably only applies to a limited number of cabins on a specific sailing date. Every ship has 6-30 categories of cabin.

Your 'no fly' cruise specialist is there to provide you with the very best price available for the cruise that you want.

10   'Credit Hold'. Some Cruise Lines ask passengers to complete a form to authorise their credit card. They will then hold the estimated total amount per passenger for each day of the cruise on your card and so the credit amount held is quite high. This can limit the credit facility on your card, regardless of whether you have spent that total or not.

If this is a problem talk to the hotel manager and they can usually reduce the amount held to a more realistic level dependent on your spending patterns up to that point.

11   'Guaranteed Exchange rate'. This is a rate some Cruise Lines use if the currency of payment is different from the ships currency. The guaranteed rate can be higher than the rate quoted by the banks, making purchases and settling your cabin account higher than expected.

Most UK 'no fly' cruises are on ships whose standard onboard currency is Sterling. For those that are not, or for spending money on excursions, it is often better to purchase your currency in advance.

12 Extra Gratuities. Some major Cruise Lines automatically imprint an additional gratuities line on signed receipts for such things as spa treatments, extra cost coffees, bar charges etc. despite a 15% gratuity already being added. So offering you the chance to pay double gratuity.

Remember - don't add a tip on top of a gratuity (unless you want to!)

13 The cost of bottled mineral water to take on excursions is expensive and don't forget there will still be an additional gratuity of 15%

It is often cheaper to buy soft drinks and water onshore than it is onboard.

14 The cost of bingo cards! One Cruise Line is now charging £26 for a block of four cards.

If you enjoy Bingo then discuss this with your 'no fly' cruise specialist and they can advise you which ships are the best and cheapest for this activity.

15 On arrival in your cabin a bottle of water is on display for your 'convenience' which will then cost you £3.50. Also a waiter handing out drinks when you arrive will charge you £4.50 for a drink full of ice worth £1.00.

Take a couple of bottles of water with you for use whilst embarking (which can take some time) and for immediate use in your cabin - that first drink is often the most expensive!

16 Formal seating for dinner. As tables are normally set up for four, six or eight people you could be seated with passengers who you find you have nothing in common with.

Don't suffer in silence - if you want to change tables then discuss this with the restaurant manager - a small gratuity and a smile is often all it takes to get the table you want!

The 10 classic objections to cruising

1.   I'll get bored
Cruising can be as relaxed or as active as you wish. With the new resort-style ships there is really no excuse to be bored, as the variety and scope of the facilities and activities on offer would be difficult to replicate on any land-based alternative.

2.   It's only for old people
Many of the new cruise ships are designed to appeal to the younger market and families with children. Indeed the fastest growing sector of the cruise industry is the family market.

3.   It's too formal
This is a very outdated image that experienced cruisers have long recognised as not being true. Many of the new ships have created a distinctly less formal atmosphere and although some ships still have 'formal' nights the dress requirement is more relaxed and if this isn't for you then many ships operate a casual dining experience.

4.   It's claustrophobic
This may have been true on some older ships, but this could not be further from the truth nowadays. But if you do suffer from this then outside cabins and staterooms with balconies offer the entire sea to look out on to.

5.   I'm forced to socialise with people I don't know
Many ships have open seating restaurants which allow you to dine when, where and with whom you wish. But many cruisers enjoy the sociable aspect of cruising and return with new found friends each time they sail away.

6.   There's too much food
Well, this is certainly true, but many ships also have state of the art leisure and exercise facilities and so now you can have the best of both worlds!

7.   The journey to the departure port is too far
That is the benefit of 'no fly' cruising – you depart from and return to a UK port, often close to home.

8.   I'll get seasick
All modern ships are highly stabilised and the incidence of seasickness is now rare. But if you do suffer then over the counter seasickness remedies are often effective.

9.   It's expensive
Cruising has never represented such good value for money. Remember that when comparing prices that the cost of a cruise includes your accommodation, all food,

entertainment and most on-board facilities and activities. So break the price down to a 'per day' cost and you can begin to appreciate the great value available.

10. There's too much choice – it's too confusing

There's the old adage that 'choice can be a blessing or a curse' and from our experience there are many prospective cruisers that are turned off the idea because the very act of selecting and purchasing a cruise appears to be so daunting.

The market is confusing, but there are specialists here to help you and so if you are looking for a 'no fly' cruise then a 'no fly' cruise specialist will be able to lead you through the maze. And remember, with so much choice comes variety and the opportunity to find the perfect cruise to suit you.

Frequently Asked Questions

ABTA

There are many different ways of buying a cruise today so it is very important that you book your cruise from a company that is a member of ABTA.

ABTA ensures the money that you've paid for your cruise is safe if the travel company you've dealt with goes out of business. ABTA can also help if something goes wrong with your travel arrangements and you're unable to resolve the problem with your ABTA travel company. Members of ABTA must adhere to a Code of Conduct which ensures you receive a high standard of service, fair terms of trading, and accurate information on issues such as passports and visas, health requirements and details of any alterations to your holiday.

Activities & facilities on board

This can vary depending on the Cruise Line but most ships have a wide selection of day time activities which range from fully equipped fitness gyms, exercise and dance classes some even have rock climbing walls. For the less active passengers there are spas, cookery classes as well as the decks where you can relax and read a good book. The activities are endless and you can do as much or as little as you choose.

Anniversaries and celebrations

All cruise ships have special celebration packs and gifts available to purchase to help you celebrate any special occasion such as a birthday or anniversary. On some cruise ships you can even get married by the Captain or renew your vows. Cruise Lines will vary as to what they offer onboard to help you celebrate your special occasion.

Cabins - inside v outside

An inside cabin means you have a cabin on the inside of the ship which has no window or port hole, whilst an outside cabin is on the outside of the ship so you will have a view outside or have a balcony.

Whatever cabin type you choose, all passengers have full use of all the facilities onboard the ship. Outside cabins and balcony cabins cost more than inside cabins and are usually larger in size.

What is a guaranteed cabin?

When you book the cruise the price you pay will depend on the category of cabin so this will be guaranteed. Some Cruise Lines will assign the actual cabin number at the time of booking while others will assign when you check in.

Crime

Crime can occur on ships just like anywhere else so take the same precautions as you would at home or on any other holiday. Don't leave your room key and money on the lounge chair while you go to the bathroom, lock all valuables in the safe and lock your cabin. The number of cameras and security officers onboard has been increased. These cameras are monitored by security officials who can observe and react to any incidents which occur. When the ship is in dock you'll be security checked whenever you disembark and return to the ship and passengers are normally given photo ID cards on check-in, which you must show to enter and exit the ship. Cruise Lines, ships and the ports are required by law to have appropriate security plans.

The deployment of security staff is usually discreet so you may never notice them, but there will be trained security personnel on board at all times. If you are victim of any crime you should report this to a crew or staff member immediately. Security personnel will then inform the appropriate authorities.

Disabled passengers

Most cruise ships are accessible for people with most types of disabilities. Ships built in the last 10 years will have the most up to date suites/cabins and accessible onboard facilities. When booking a cruise always ensure that your 'no fly' cruise specialist knows of any disability so they can book the most suitable cabin and arrange any special requirements for your cruise.

Dining options

This can vary from Cruise Line and ship. Some offer 'flexible' eating and 'open' seating which means you can eat and sit where you want within the opening hours of the dining room. Depending on the size of the ship you may have one, two or four sittings as dining rooms invariably cannot accommodate all passengers at one time. More traditional ships have two sittings in their formal dining rooms, which differ only by time: typically 6:00 p.m. and 8:30 p.m. To choose, just decide whether you prefer to dine early or late. Alternative dining may also be available but this will incur an extra cost.

Dress Code

As a general guideline cruise ships class formal for men as a Dinner Jacket or dark suit, with tie and for the ladies an evening gown or cocktail dress. But don't buy a Dinner Jacket just for the trip, even on the most formal of ships; a dark suit and tie are fine for the dressiest occasions plus many ships offer Dinner Jacket rental services.

Informal for men is long trousers, a collared shirt and tie and for the ladies a dress or smart attire. Casual / relaxed for a man is long trousers with tie optional and for ladies a more casual dress or outfit.

Formal evenings
Formal evenings are all part of the fun of cruising, especially the Captain's Cocktail Party. It is acceptable for gentleman to wear a dark suit instead of a Dinner Jacket and ladies to wear cocktail dresses.

Insurance
When choosing an insurance company to cover your travel and cancellation protection always pay close attention to the terms of the insurance, particularly in the areas of 'pre-existing medical conditions' and the level of cover for lost valuables. When taking out travel insurance make sure that it covers your particular needs and ensure that it is under-written by a reputable company.

Mobiles / Internet - Keeping in touch
New ships all have the technology to enable passengers to use their own personal mobile telephone with the cost being charged to the mobile account. But beware this can be expensive. Most ships will also have internet cafes so you can send e-mails; this option is a lot less expensive than calling from your mobile phone.

Norovirus
Norovirus is not a "cruise ship" only virus. It is associated more with cruise travel simply because health officials are required to track illnesses on ships (whereas they are not at hotels and resorts); therefore, when outbreaks are found they are reported more quickly at sea than on land. Cruise ships do everything possible to prevent an outbreak by enforcing strict hygiene rules with staff and food. Symptoms are nausea, vomiting and diarrhoea and typically last only 24 to 48 hours where you will be asked to stay in your cabin so the virus does not spread to other passengers.

Passports
If you are a British Citizen you will need to have 6 months validity on your passport after your date of return. Children will need their own passports. British Visitor Passports are no longer valid. British Subject passport holders' requirements may differ so always check prior to travel and ensure you obtain all the necessary documentation as you could be refused travel without it.

Pregnancy
If your pregnancy is normal and healthy, cruising can make for a safe and relaxing holiday. Cruise Lines vary as to what stage of pregnancy they permit travel, but as a guideline if you are more than 23 - 28 weeks pregnant at any time during the cruise you would not be permitted to travel. You may need to produce a doctor's certificate as proof. Always check with the specific Cruise Line before booking and check your health insurance policy to make sure you'll be covered.

Singles
Cruising is one of the very best holiday options for single people. Firstly there will be many like minded people on board. Secondly, you will find your dining companions

will be single people also wishing to share the experience of the holiday. This is where friendships are made and throughout your cruise you could meet up with your new found friends in one of the many lounges or bars, on a sightseeing trip, by the pool or on one of the special single "get together" evenings. There is nothing to match a cruise for singles!

Smoking

Most ships have smoking and non-smoking sections in the public rooms and on deck. However, many dining rooms and even some entire ships are now totally smoke-free, reflecting passenger preferences. Some Cruise Lines permit smoking in cabins, but if they do most only allow this in cabins with balconies.

Special diets

Most ships can accommodate salt-free, low-carbohydrate, low cholesterol, Kosher, or other dietary preferences. However this request must be made in advance so be sure to advise your 'no fly' cruise specialist when you book your cruise.

Terrorism

Cruise ships have increased security against terrorism since September 11th and currently all passengers' bags are screened before they are allowed on the ship. Passengers' names are checked against a terrorist watch list before arriving to board. Restricted areas are also better protected and secured. For example, the bridge is secured to prevent access by unauthorised personnel. The number of cameras and security officers has also increased onboard and are monitored by security officials who can observe and react to any incidents which may occur. Many Cruise Lines have hired more security officers to conduct foot patrols on the boat to keep an eye on things. These security officers are also responsible for checking and re-checking the documentation of passengers initially boarding and re-boarding after excursions.

Transport to and / or parking at your departure port

Parking your car is normally at the passenger's expense and not included in the price of the cruise. Car parks in the ports are normally within walking distance of the passenger terminal, but if not a shuttle bus is normally provided. Ample parking spaces are available and there are allocated disabled spaces. The car park is a dedicated facility and is used only by cruise passengers so is secure. The car park is locked once the ship has departed and re-opened the day the ship arrives back in port.

Porters will be available to collect your luggage from the drop off point at the terminal and take it to your cabin for you. In some cases trolleys will be provided to help you take your luggage from your car to the drop off point. Please keep hold of your hand luggage, tickets and passport.

Please note that all vehicles are left at the owners' risk.

Valuables

Most cruise ships have safes available in cabins to put all valuable items and documents. As with any type of holiday or at home, use common sense when in public areas and do not leave any personal belongings or valuables unattended.

What's included in the price of my cruise?

What is included will depend on the cruise company you book with. As a general rule all the food and entertainment will be included in the fare, some may also include gratuities and others offer an all inclusive package which includes all your drinks. Port charges and taxes are also included in the fare.

What to pack

This will depend on the cruise ship and the itinerary. Some Cruise Lines offer a more relaxed and casual approach to dress throughout the cruise - while on others, formal dinners or parties are part of the fun. Cruise holidays are generally casual by day, whether you're on the ship or ashore, but in the evening the ship's dress codes may vary.

When booking check with your 'no fly' cruise specialist as to how many formal & informal nights there are so that you can pack accordingly.

Tips & gratuities

This can vary depending on the Cruise Line, some will include the gratuities in the price of the cruise so tips are not expected however this is still at the discretion of the passenger. Cruise ships that do not include gratuities will advise what the recommended daily amount is per passenger. Some will even add this to your onboard account.

Other suggestions to ensure a stress-free cruise

The most important things to decide is the right Cruise Line, ship size and itinerary - also consider the ship's dining options and seating arrangements. If travelling as a family check what children's facilities and activities are on board. Alternatively if you do not want to be surrounded by children check which operator offers adult only cruises. Before you travel, find out how many formal and casual nights there are onboard the cruise so you can plan your packing. Check your passport validity and make sure that any visas have been applied for in plenty of time.

When arriving on the ship get your bearings, familiarise yourself with the ship's layout and your cabin location. Decide which excursions and Spa treatments you would like and book them at the beginning of the cruise so you are not disappointed if they get fully booked. Then just relax and enjoy the cruise doing as much or as little as you like...

NoFlyCruising.com

Where to go for further information

Passenger Shipping Association

Website: www.the-psa.co.uk
Telephone: 0207 436 2449
Address: 1st Floor, 41-42 Eastcastle Street, London, W1W 8DU
Office hours: 09.00hrs to 17.30hrs, Monday to Friday

ABTA

Website: www.abta.com
Telephone: 0901 201 5050
Address: ABTA Ltd, 30 Park Street, London SE1 9EQ.
Office hours: 09.00hrs to 17.30hrs, Monday to Friday.

Passport office

Website: www.direct.gov.uk and www.fco.gov.uk
Email: info@passport.gov.uk
Telephone: Identity and Passport Service Advice line
              0300 222 0000
Office hours: 08.00hrs to 18.00hrs, Monday to Friday, and
              09.00hrs to 17.30hrs weekends

Visa Information – Home Office UK Border Agency

Website: www.ukvisas.gov.uk
Telephone: 020 7035 4848
Address: Direct Communications Unit, 2 Marsham Street, London SW1P 4DF
Office Hours: 09:00hrs to 17:00hrs, Monday to Friday

Inoculations

Contact your local GP or Medical Centre to check what inoculations you may
need to visit countries on your cruise itinerary.

Berlitz Cruising Guide

Website: www.berlitzcruising.com
Website: www.amazon.co.uk

Cut through the Cruise clutter.

www.noflycruising.com *is your single source for expert and independent advice for all 'no fly' cruises.*

Our 'no fly' cruise specialists are on hand to guide you through the cruising maze, offer you the best prices in the market and ensure that the cruise you buy is best suited to your individual requirements.

Price checker facility £££££££££

We are happy to compare prices across the whole market to ensure that you get the best deal on your cruise.

Freephone Advice Line	**Book with Confidence**	**Brochure Request Service**
Call us on **0800 458 5365** to ask any questions of our 'no fly' cruise specialists.	The company trades under an **ABTA** licence which means that your money is 100% guaranteed when you book a cruise with **NoFlyCruising.com**	Order 'no fly' brochures from Cruise Lines from one place at: **www.noflycruising.com**

To reassure you of our operating standards and expertise we are full members of ACE - the Association of Cruise Experts.

NO FLY CRUISING.com

0844 856 9471

Email: **info@noflycruising.com** Telephone: **0844 856 9471**
Coast Road, Hopton on Sea, Norfolk NR31 9BX
Office Hours: Monday to Friday: 09.00 to 17.00 – Saturdays: 09.00 to 16.00